Adult Coloring Book

30+ Stress Relieving Mandala & Geometric Flower Designs

Unique, fun, and creative artist-drawn adult coloring pages perfect for stress relief, self-care and mindfulness.

Drawn, Designed & Created by Max Miner

Copyright © 2018 Maxwell Miner

All Rights Reserved

Dedicated - To You

This coloring book is for everyone trying to find a balance and moment of relief from stress in this crazy chaotic modern world of ours.

I myself have struggled with stress and anxiety for much of my life and the act of drawing and creating these color pages for you is my own form of stress relief drawing/art.

ISBN-13: 978-1727100860 // **ISBN-10:** 1727100867

Thank You!

Thank you for supporting my work by purchasing a copy of my adult coloring book.

I hope you enjoy coloring these pages as much as I have enjoyed creating them.

See below for more information about bonus extras and where to find more of my work.

Bonus Coloring Pages

To show my thanks, I have included 3 BONUS COLORING PAGES at the back to give you an exclusive sneak peek at several upcoming coloring books I will be releasing in the near future!

Follow Me & My Work

Find Me Elsewhere:

Online Store --- **Shop.MxMnr.com**

Etsy Shop --- **Etsy.com/MaxMinerOfficialArt**

Portfolio Website --- **MaxMiner.com**

Instagram --- **@MaxMiner_OfficialArt**

Share Your Work

Tag me on Instagram! I always like to see the amazing creations people make with my work.

If you post your coloring creations on social, tag me and I'll help promote and support it!

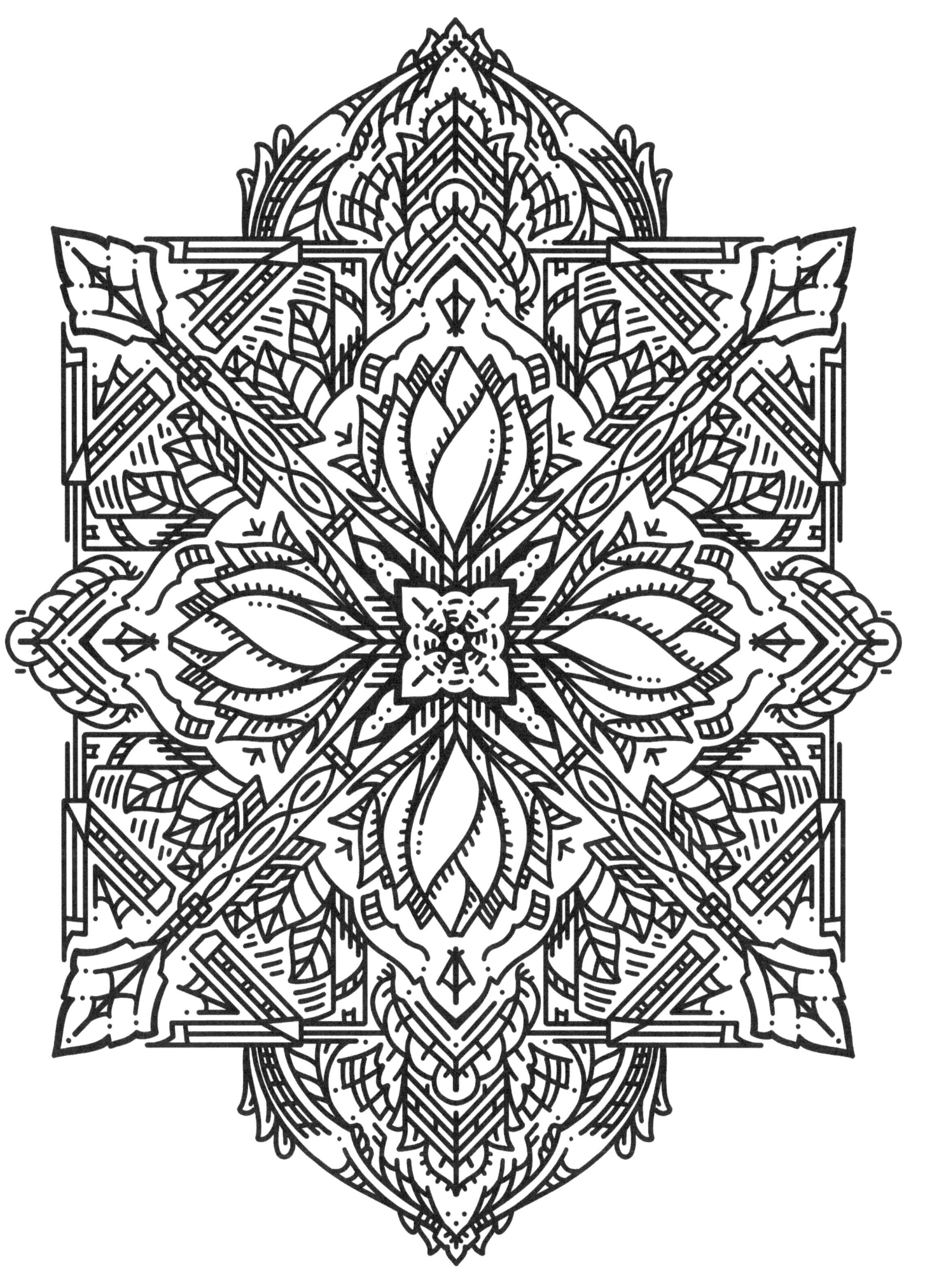

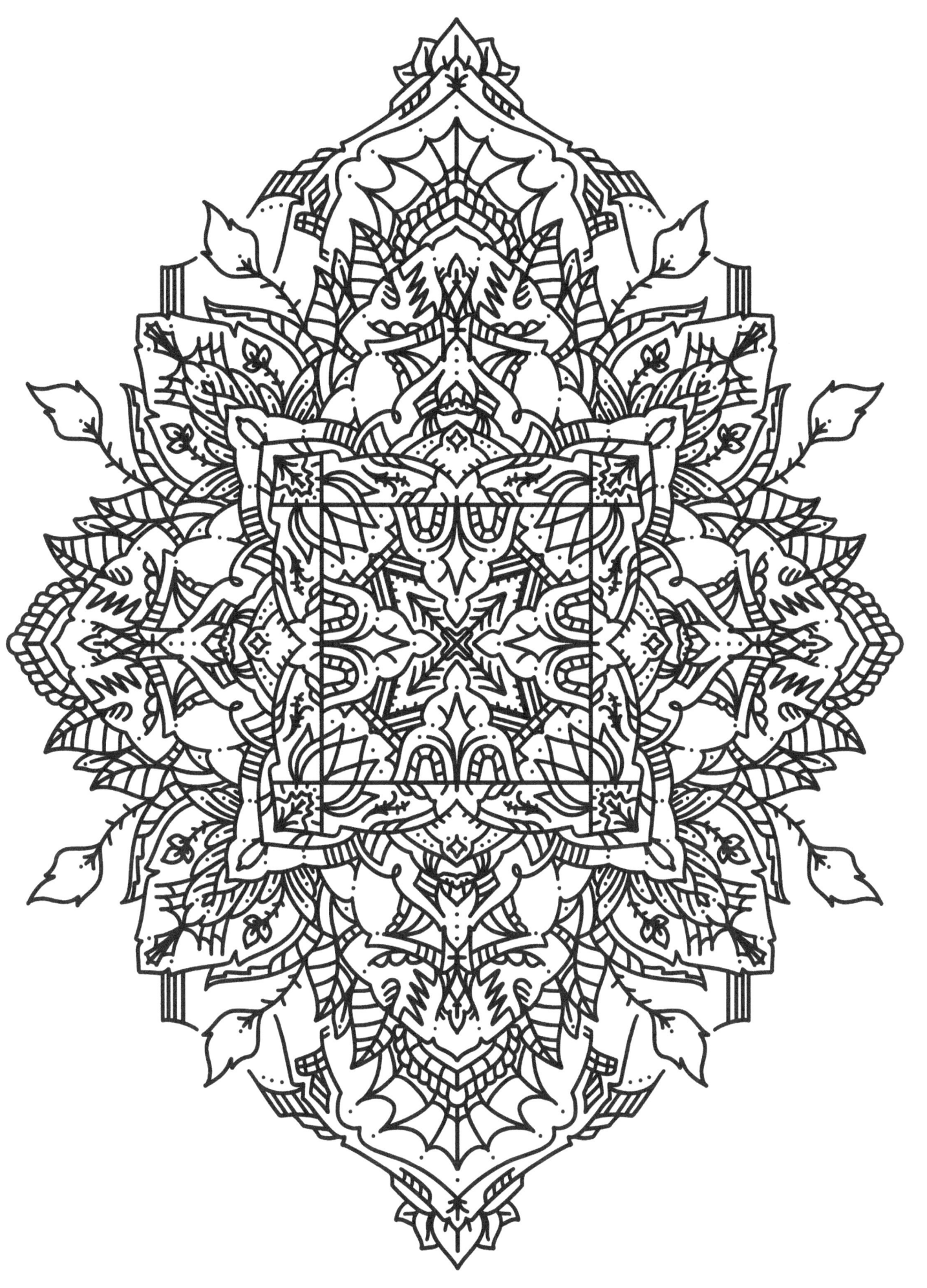

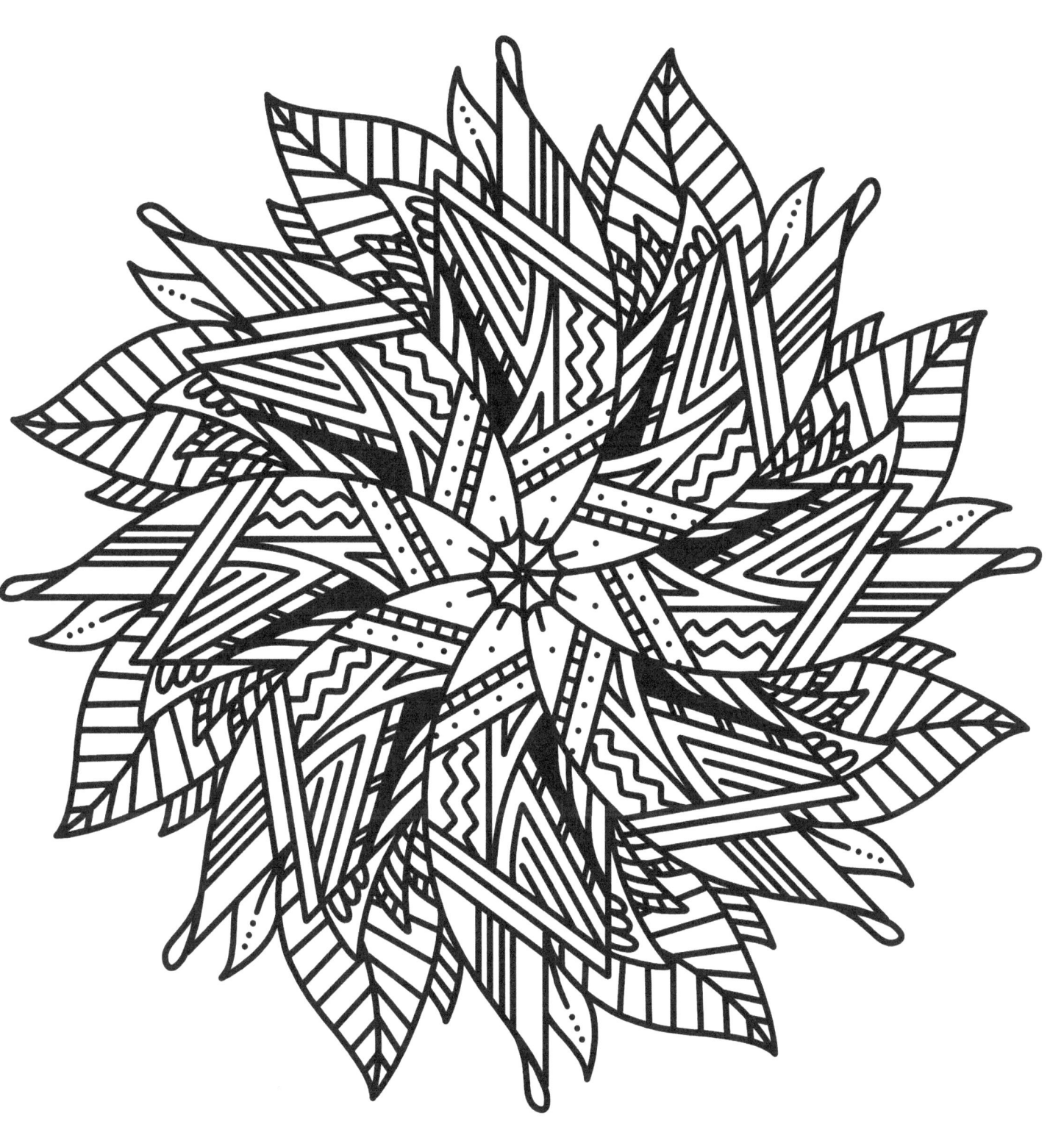

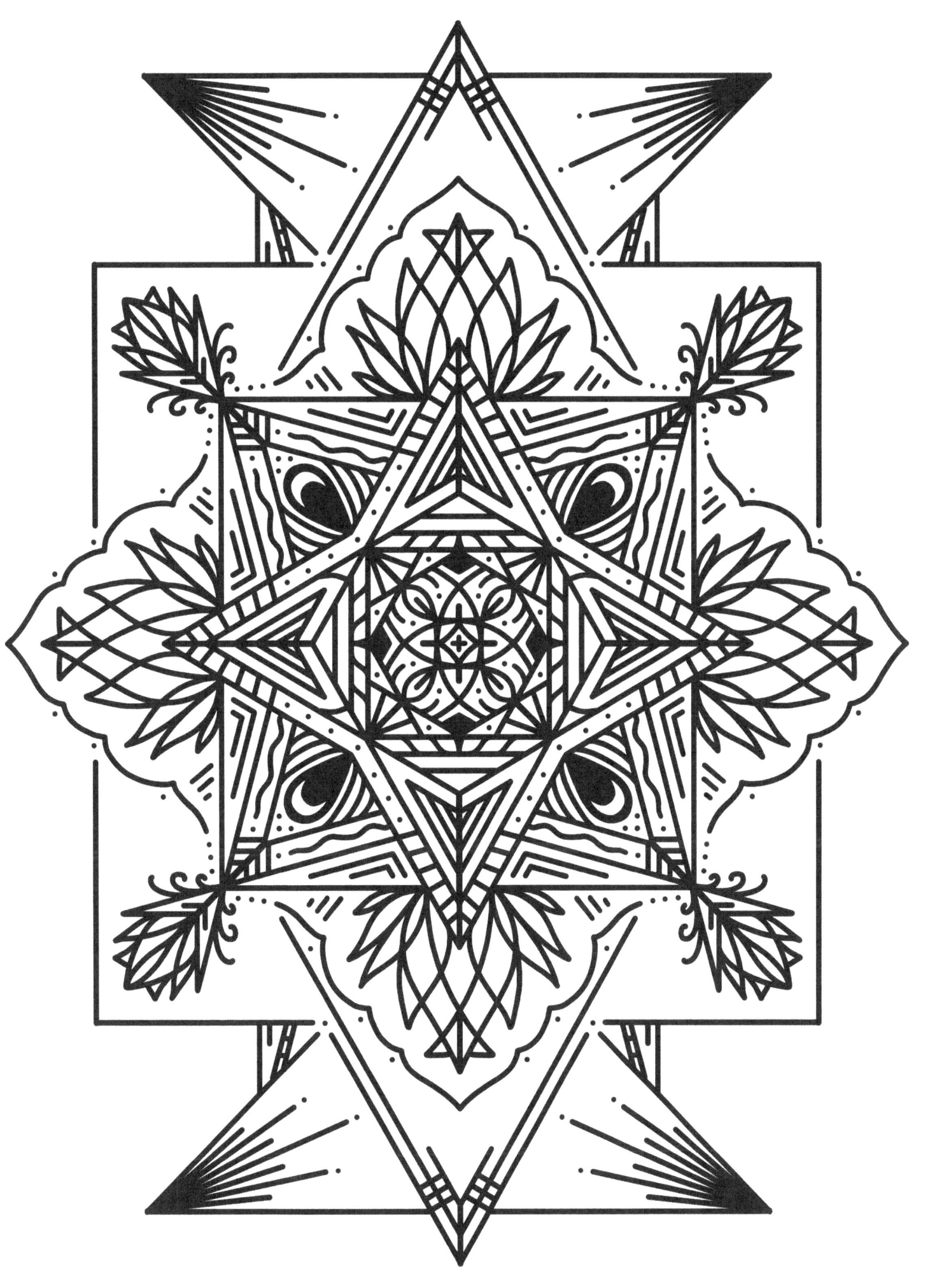

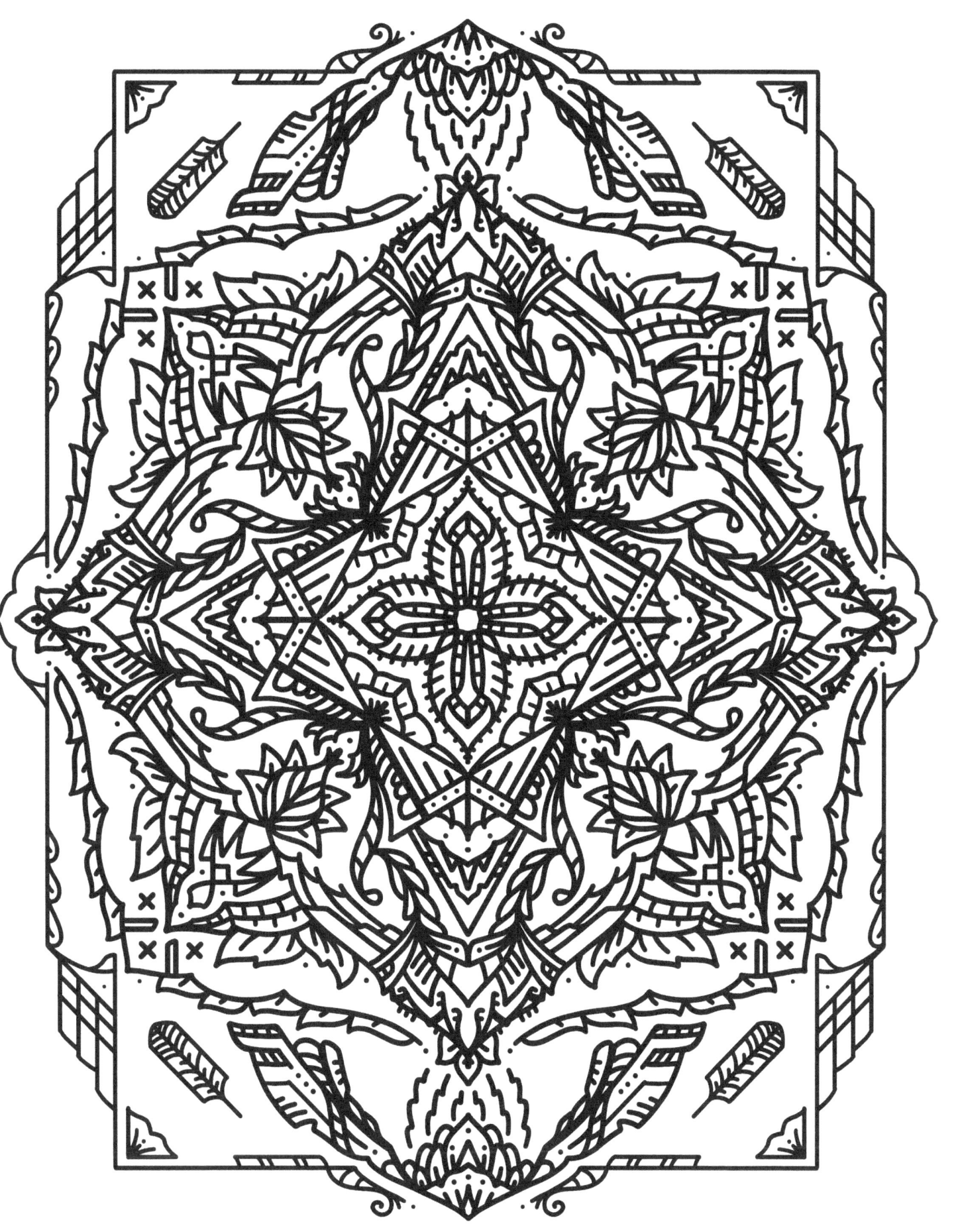

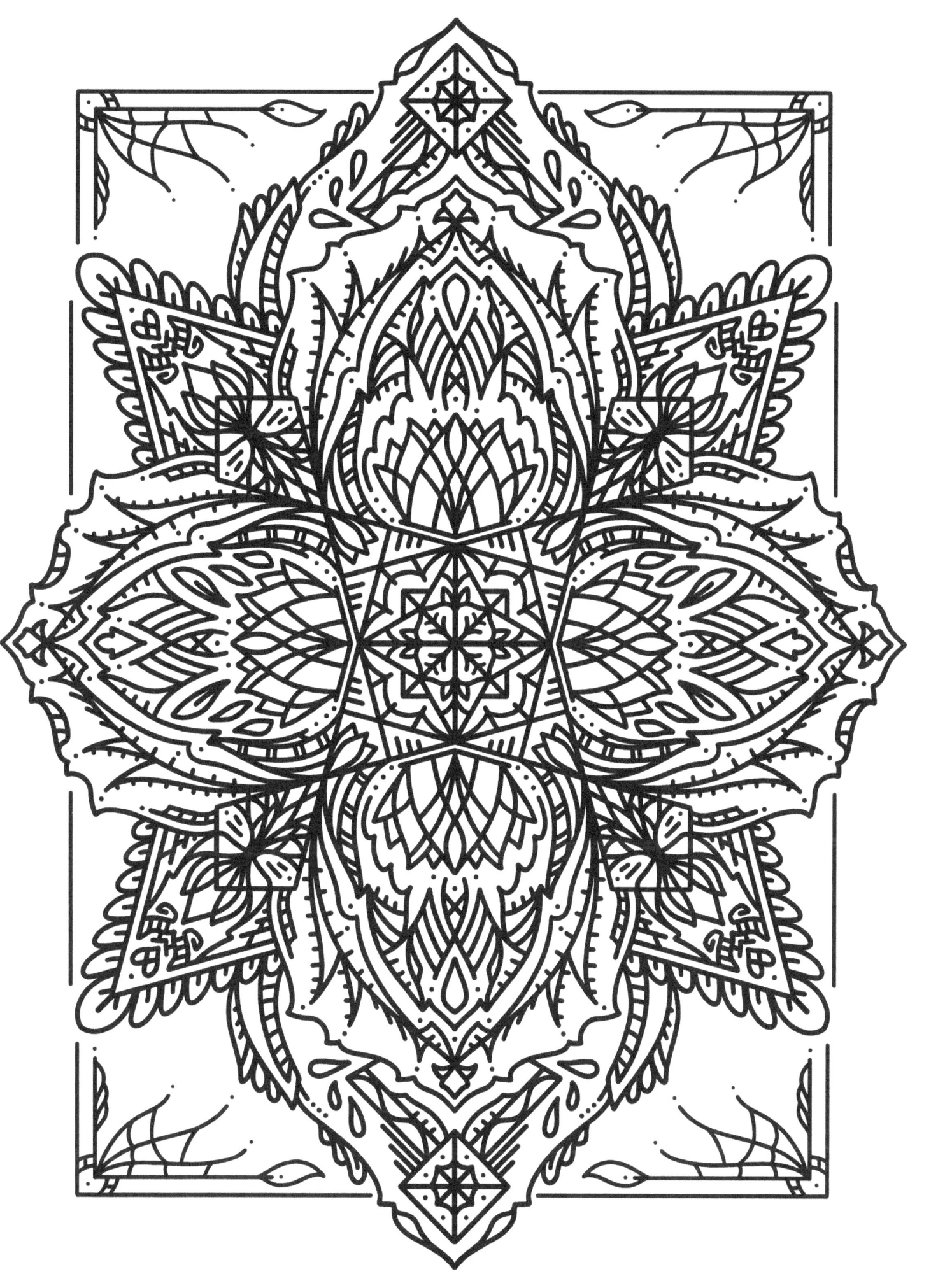

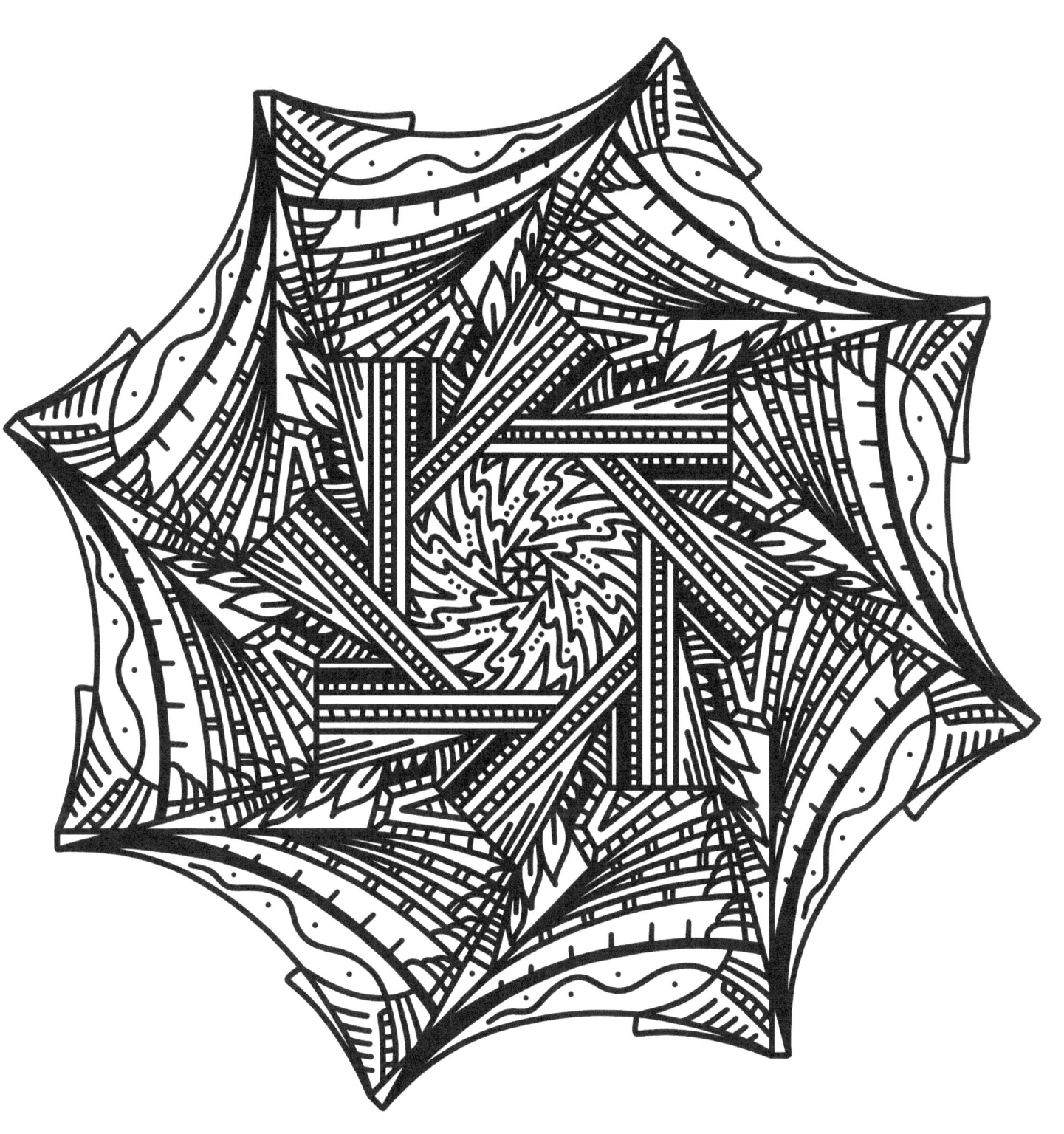

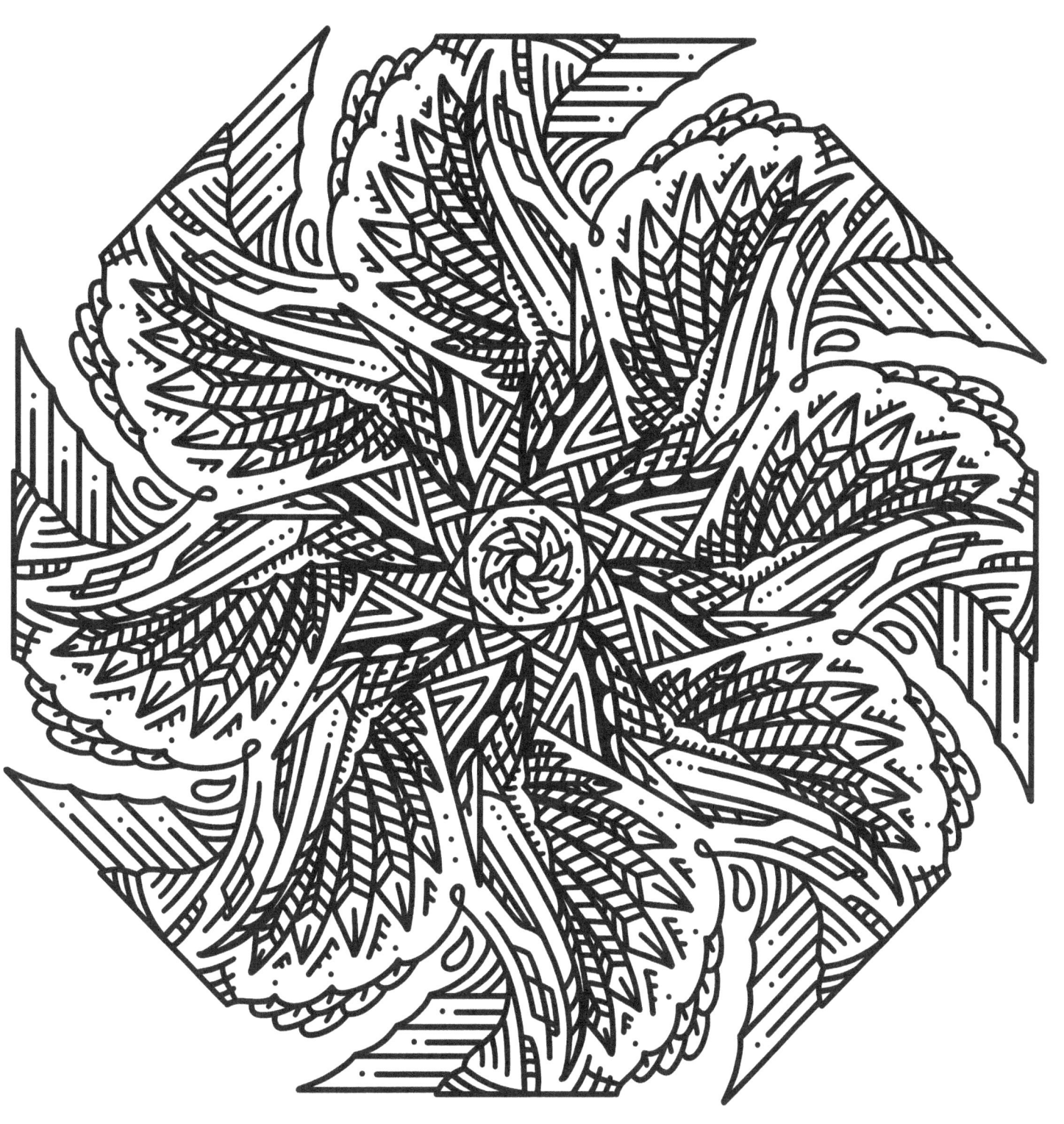

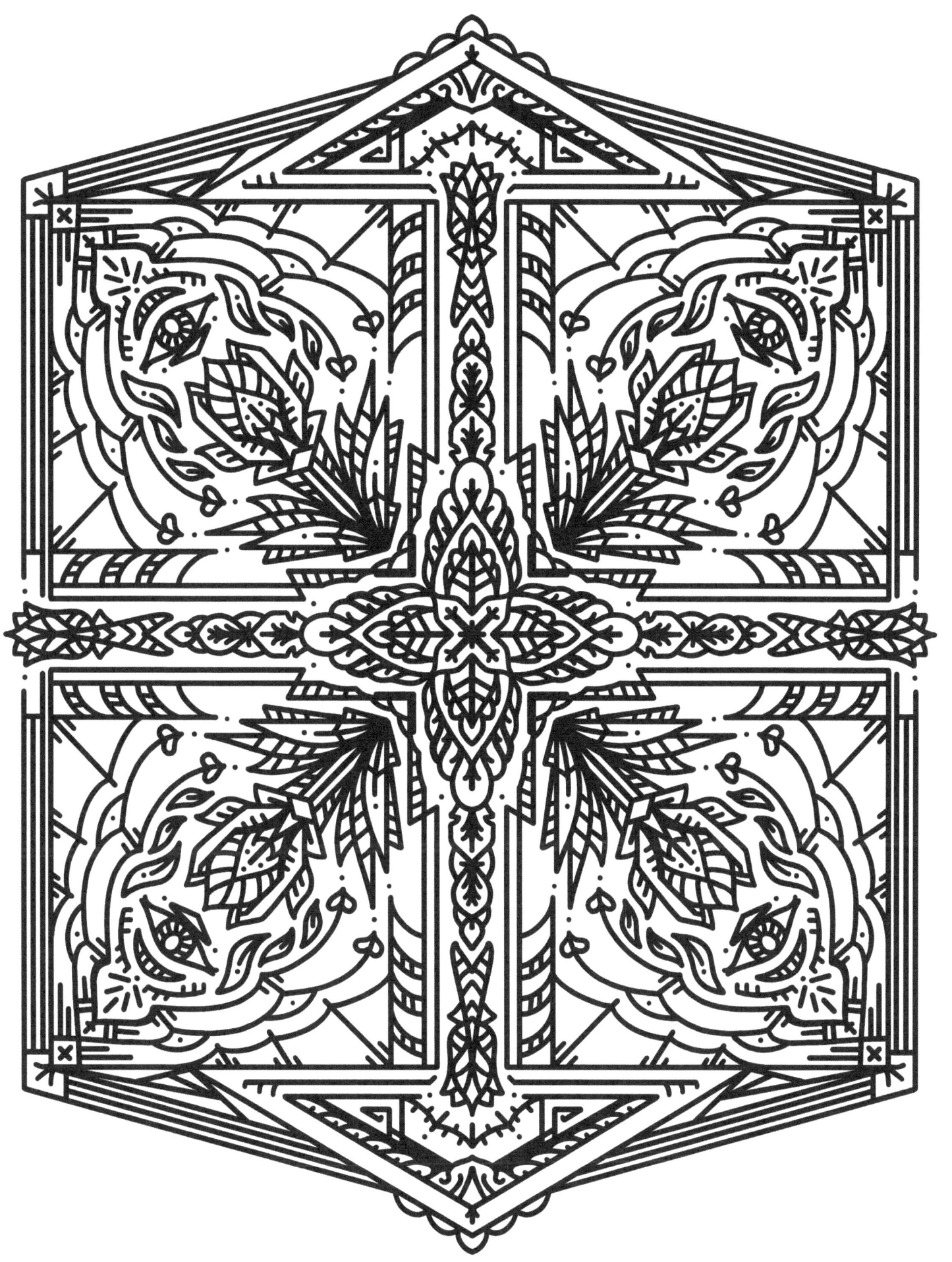

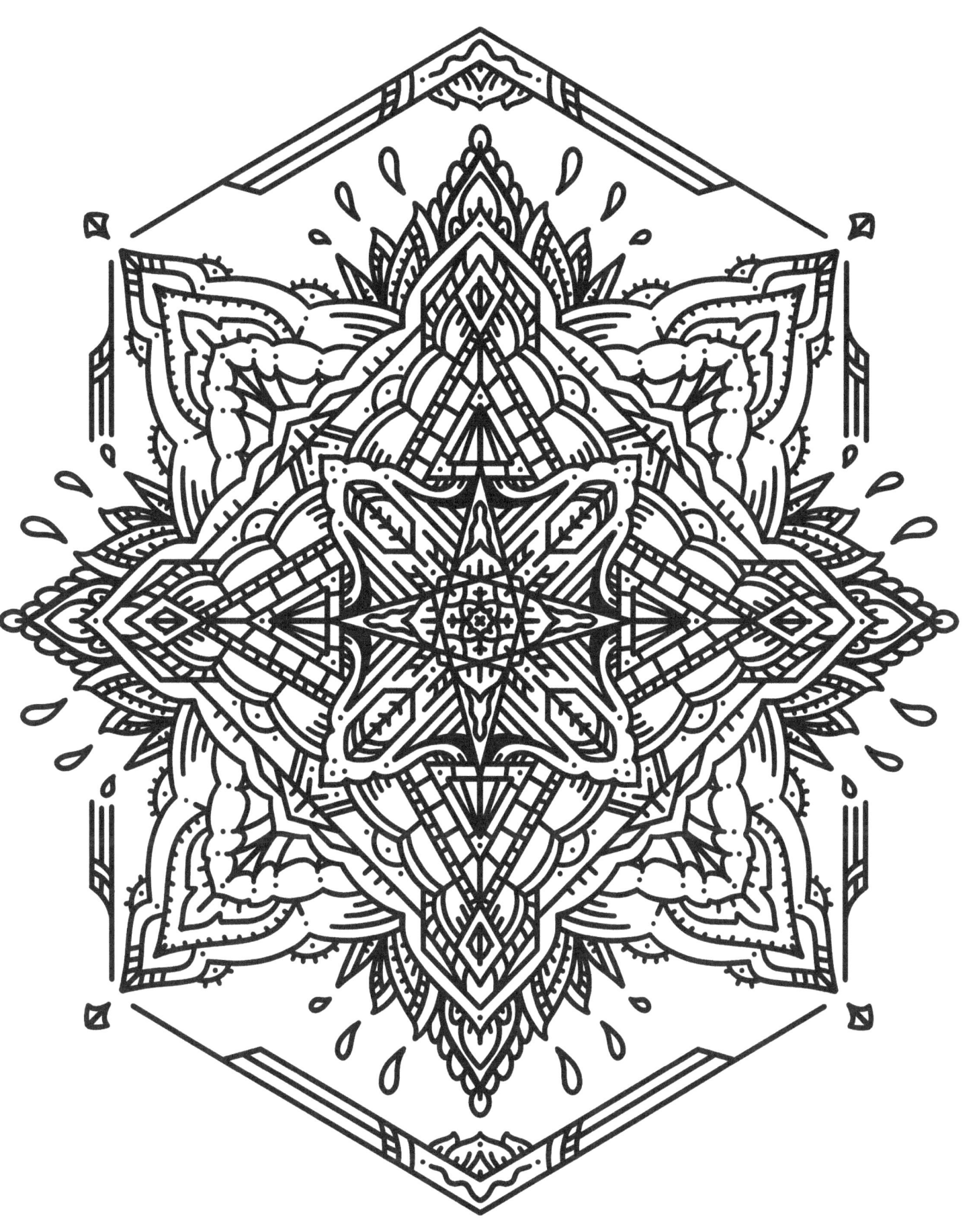

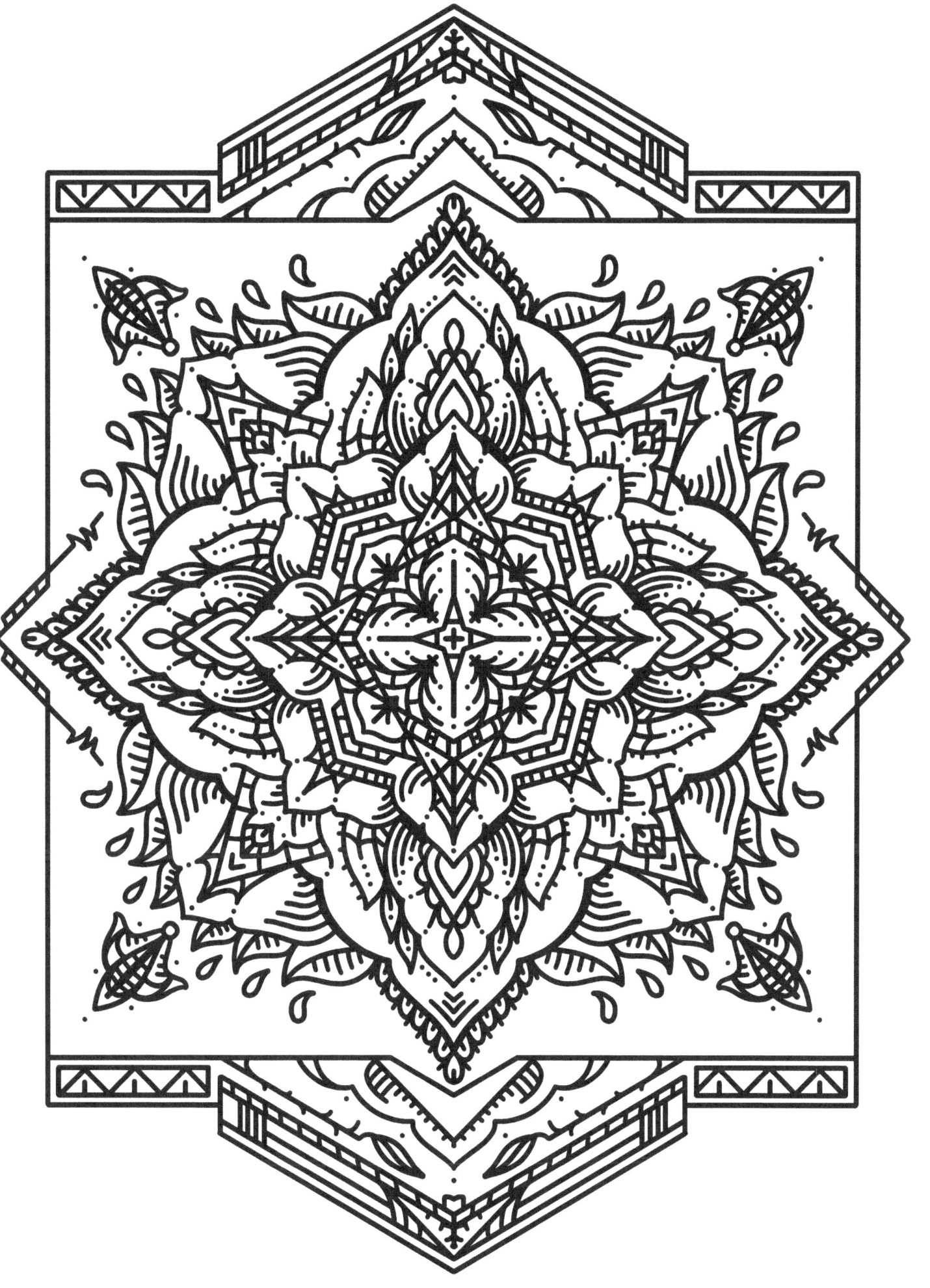

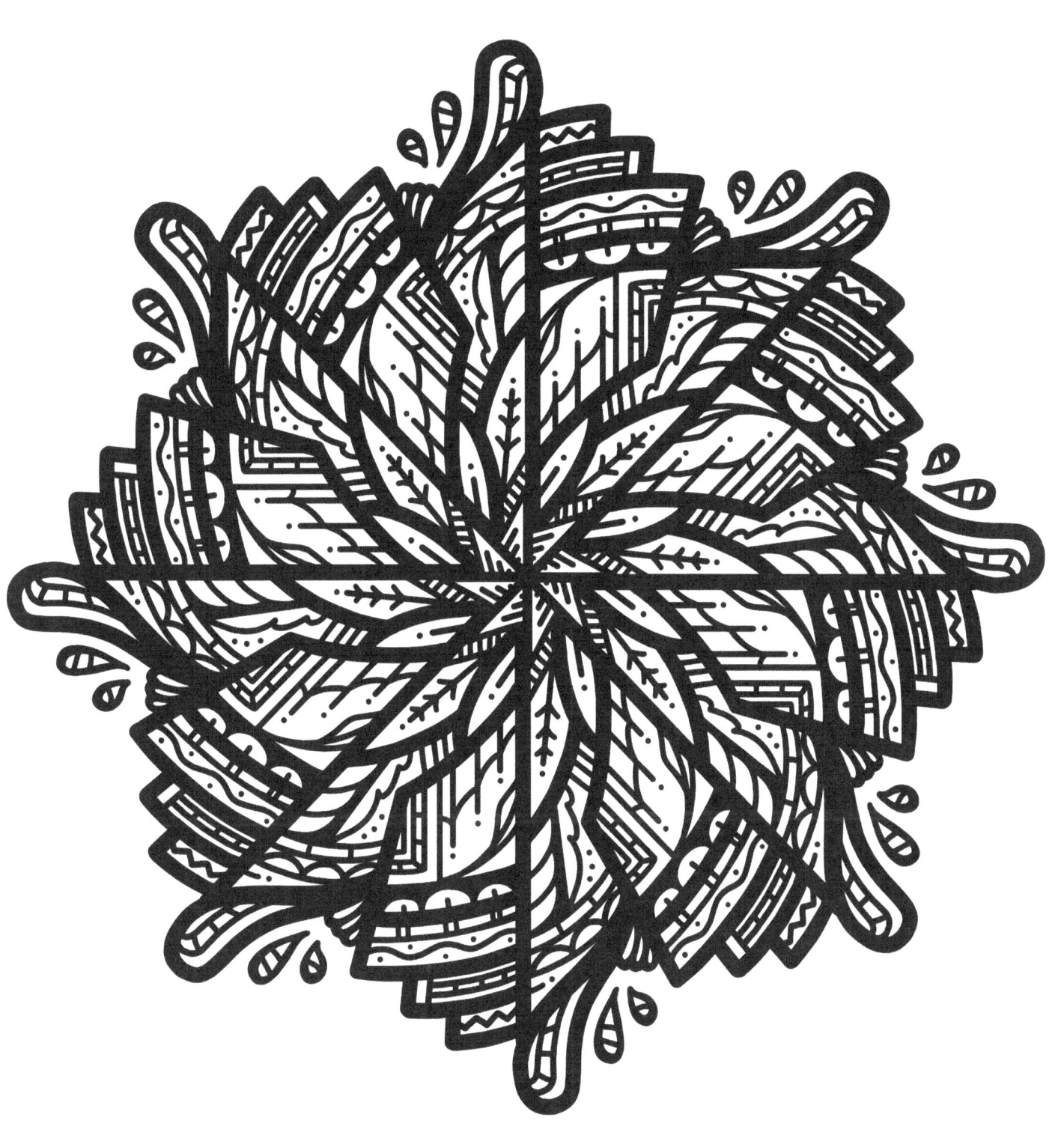

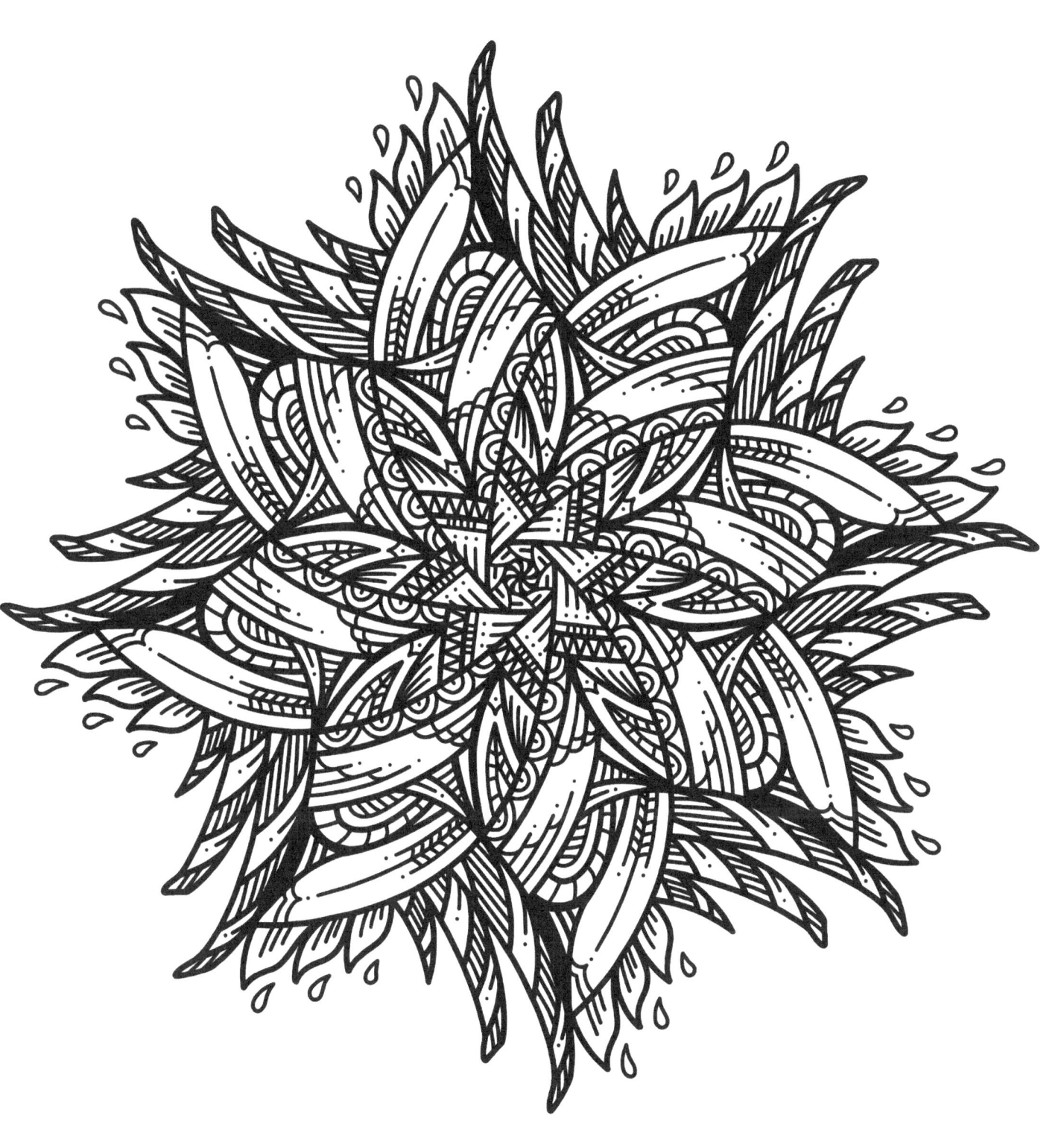

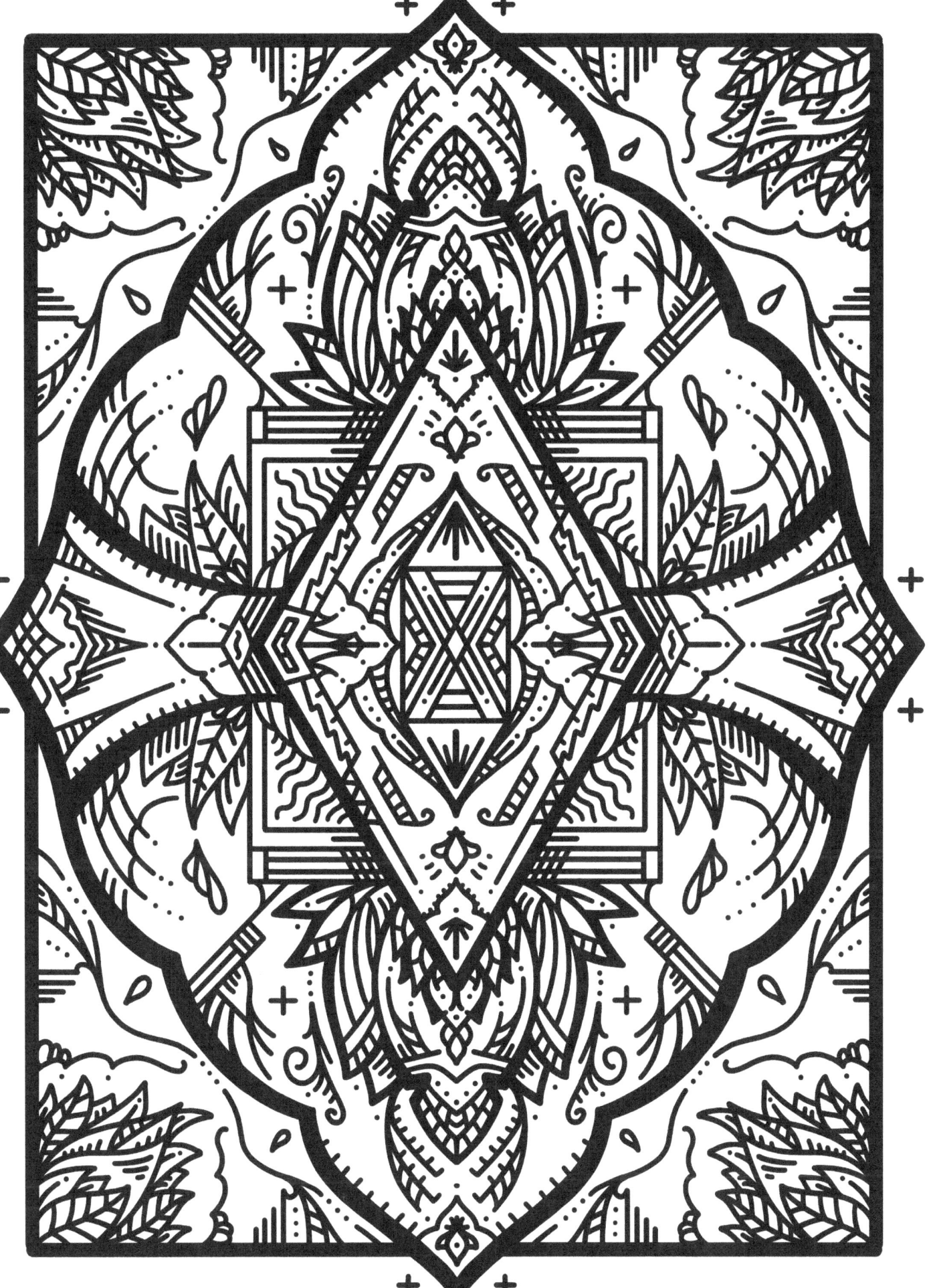

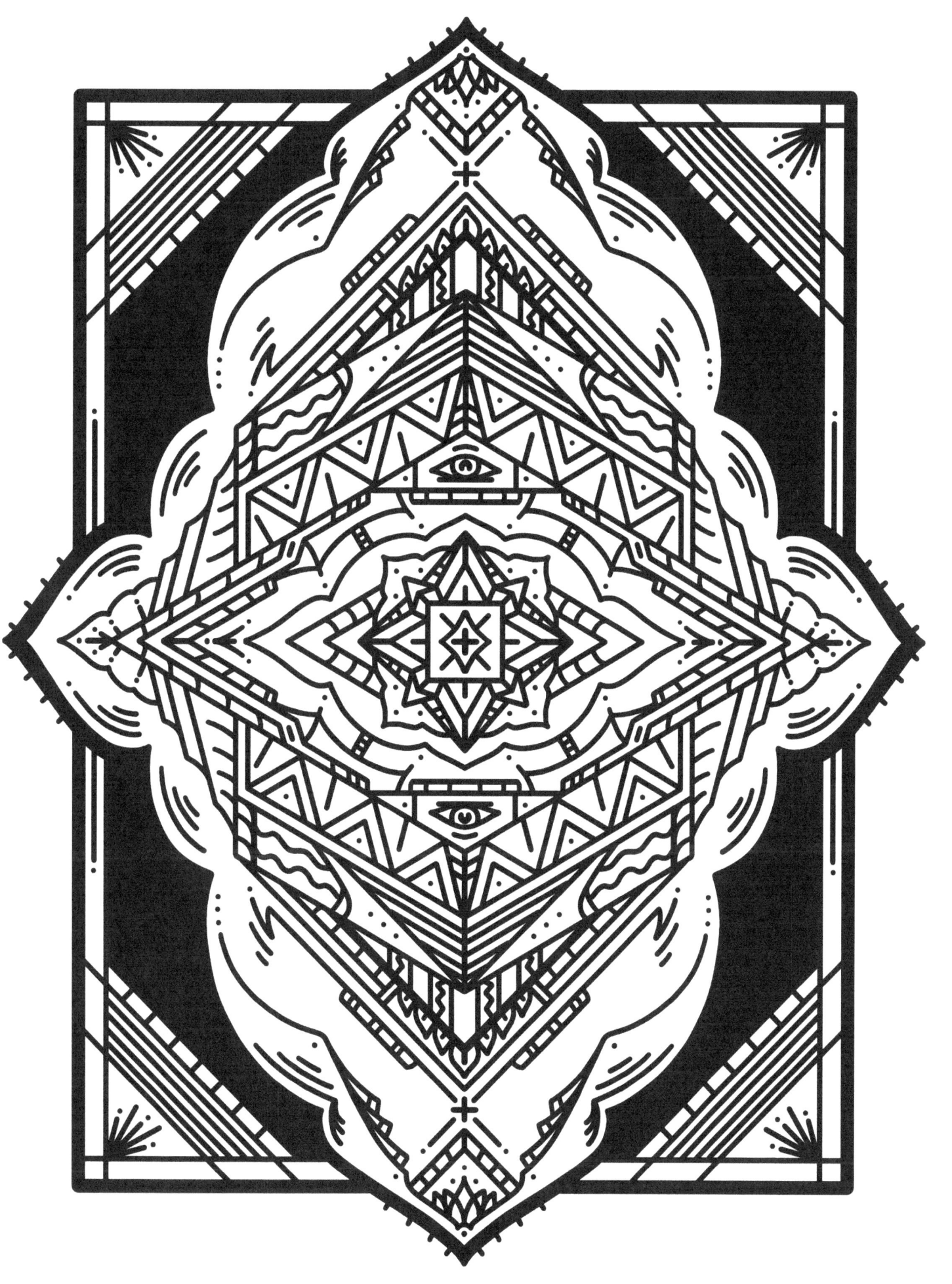

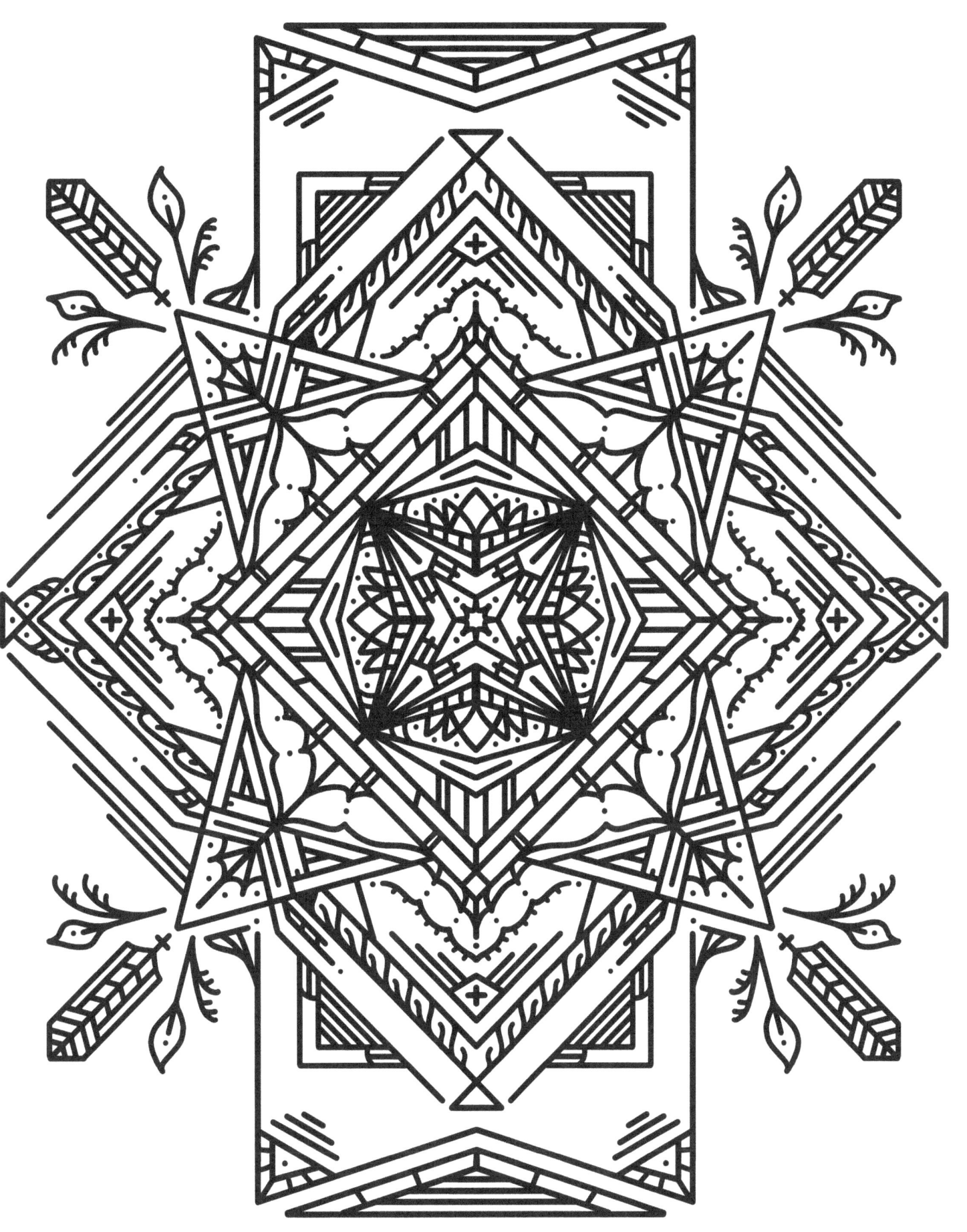

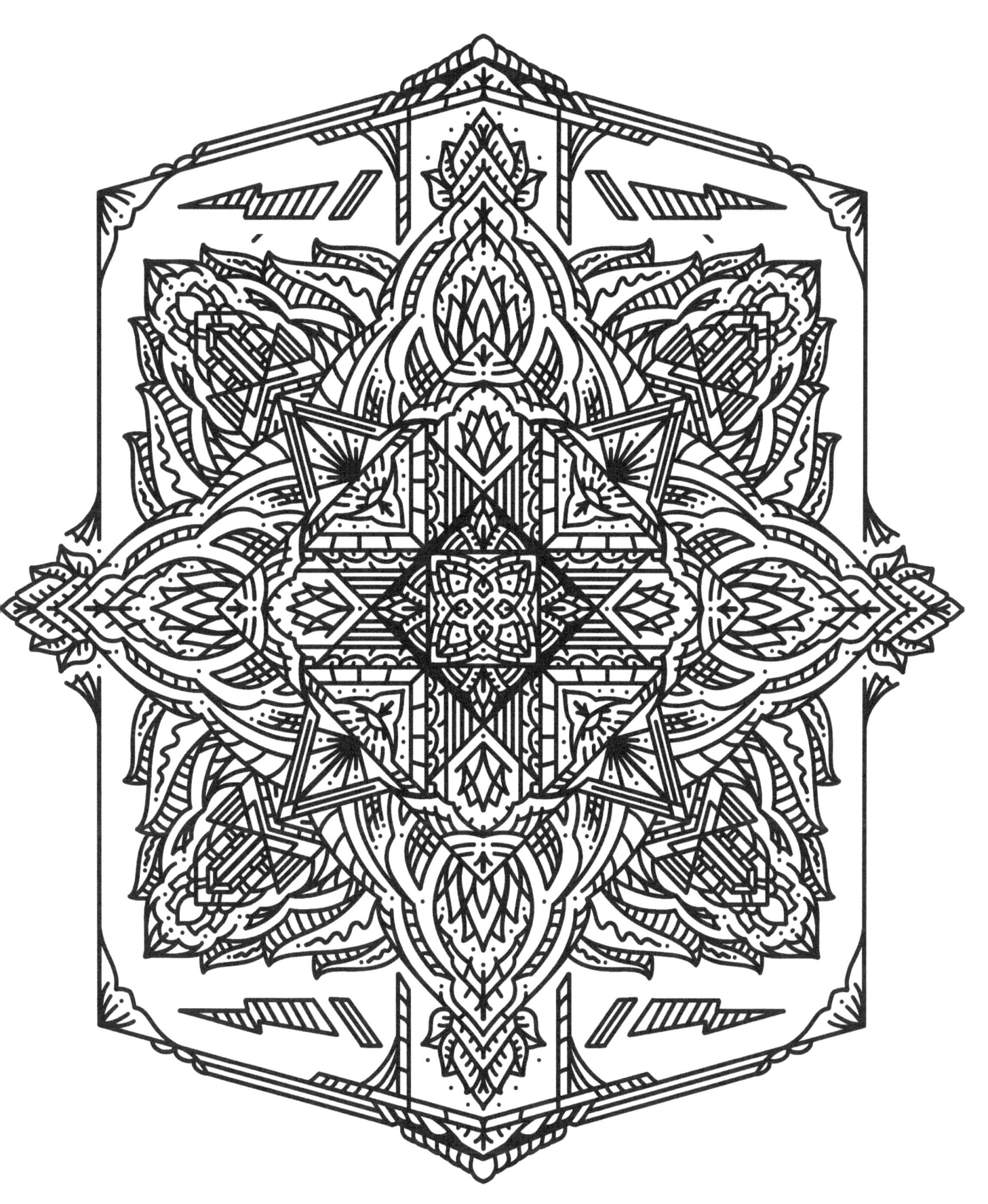

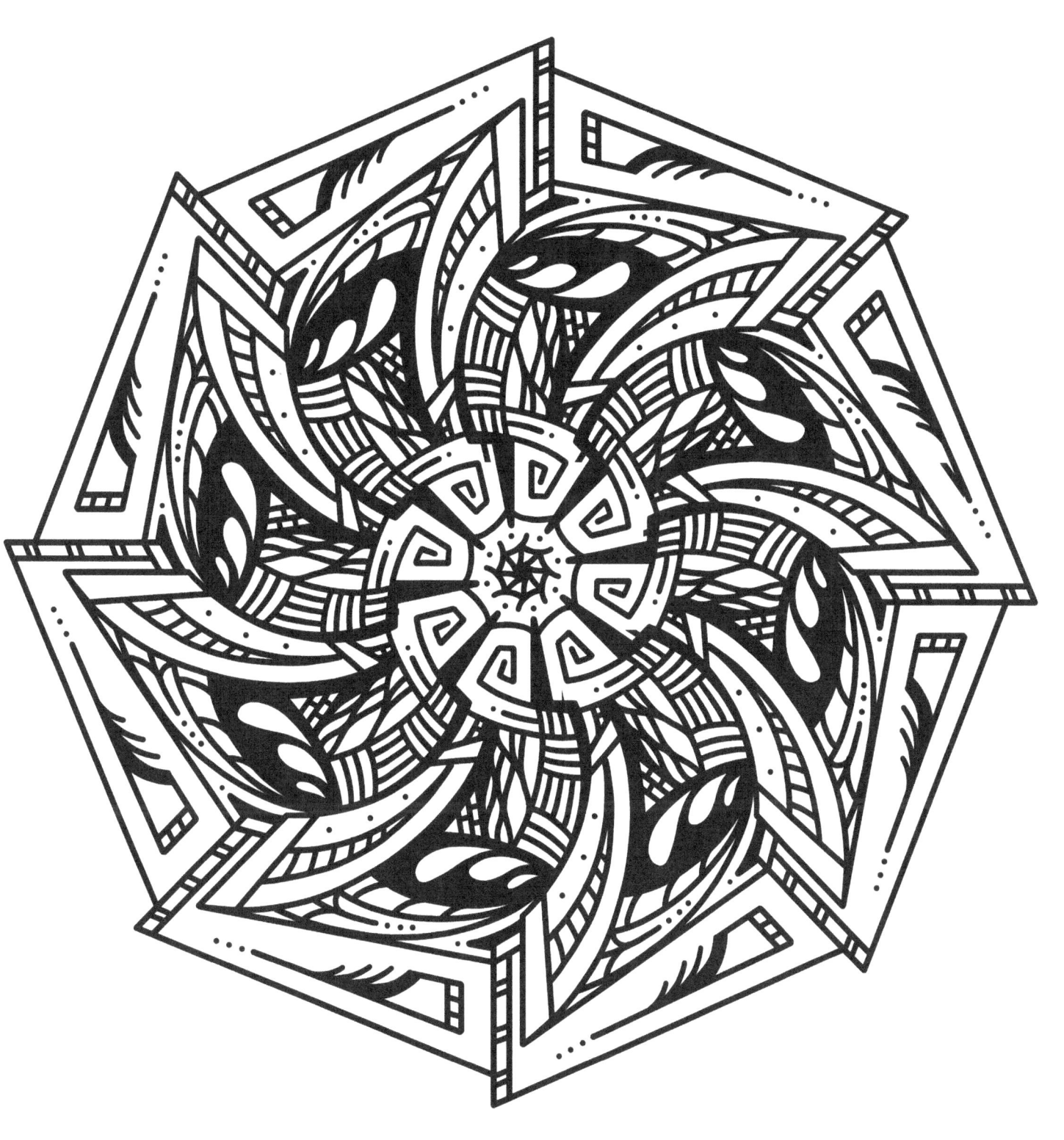

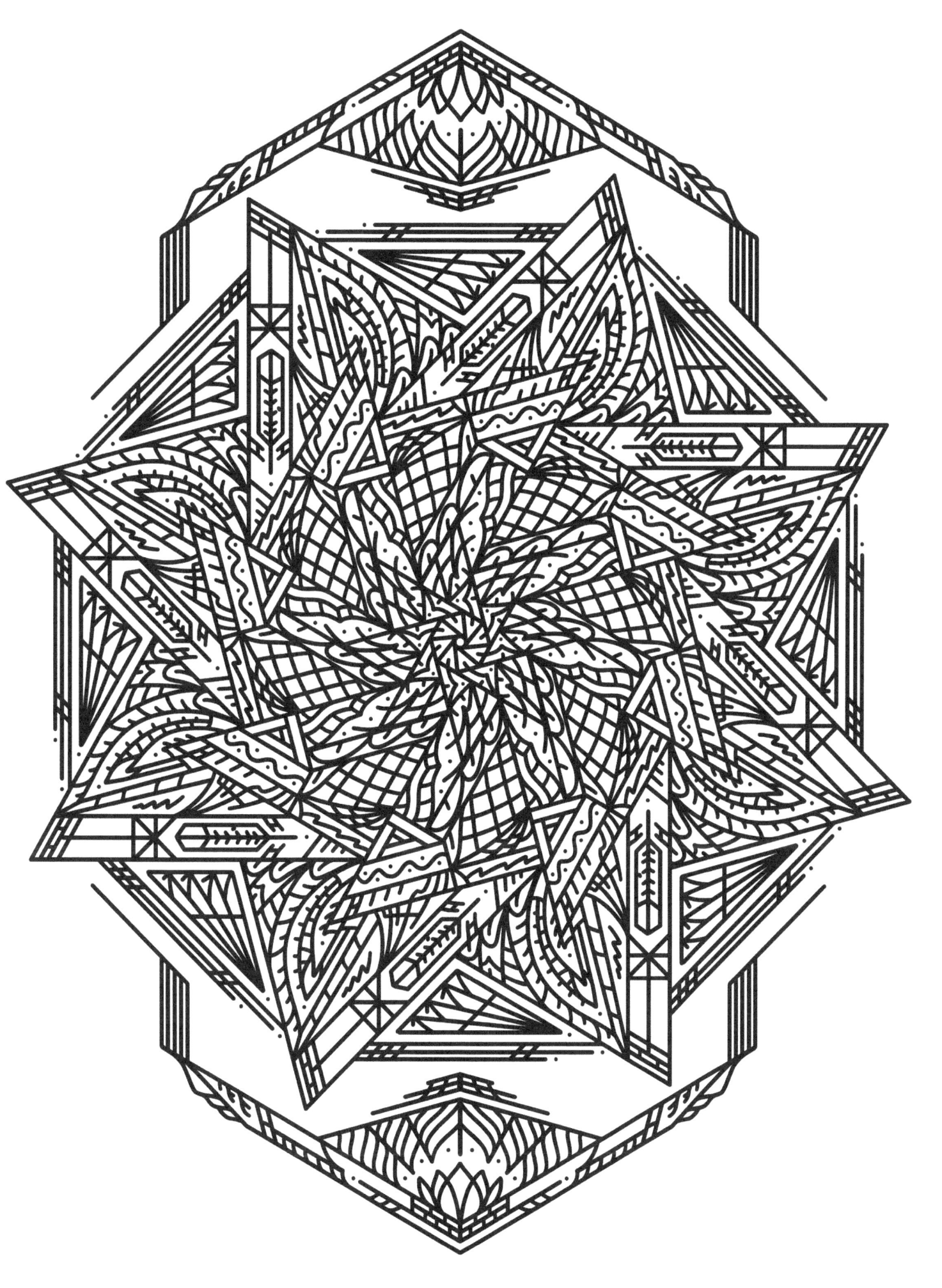

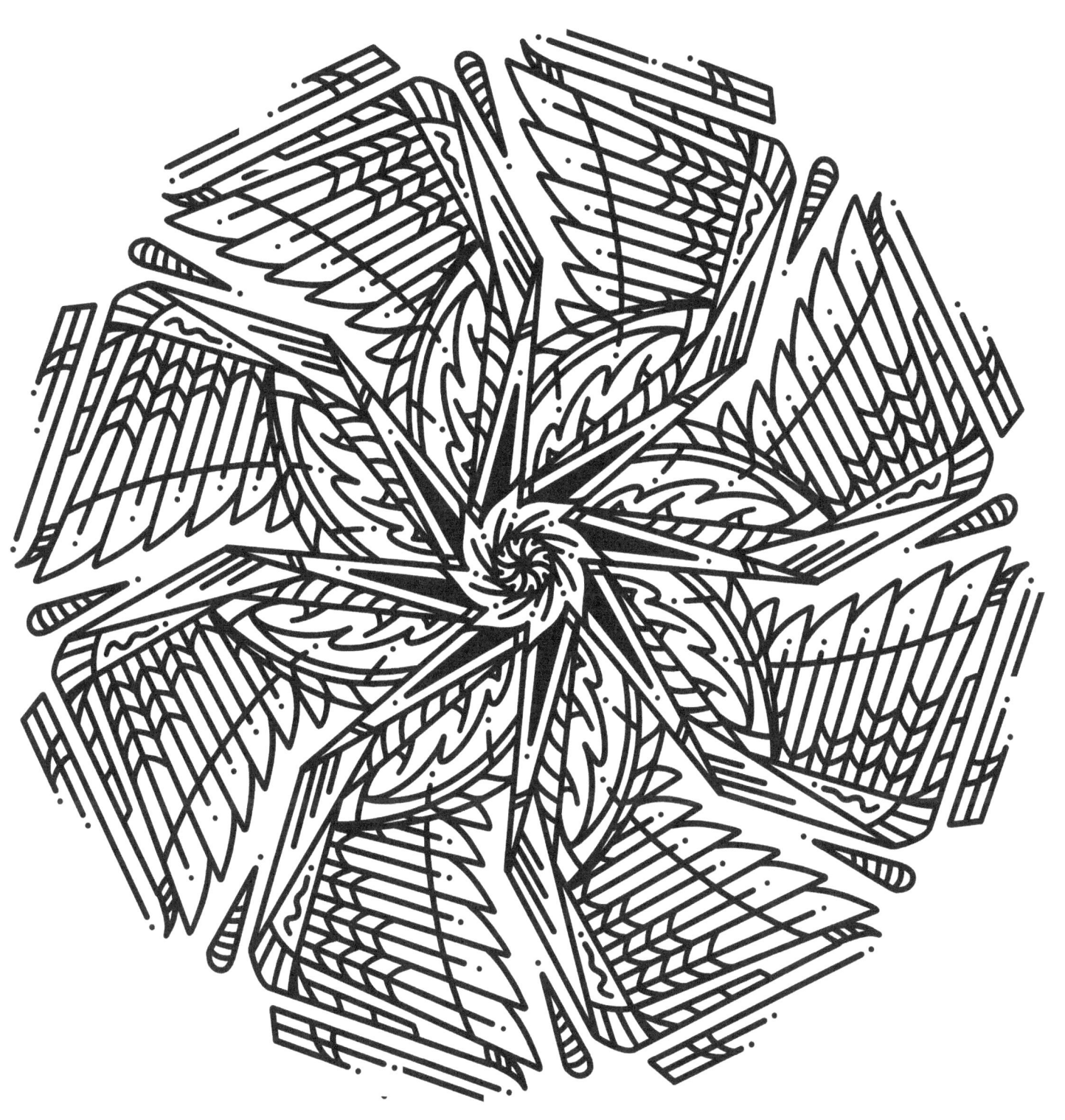

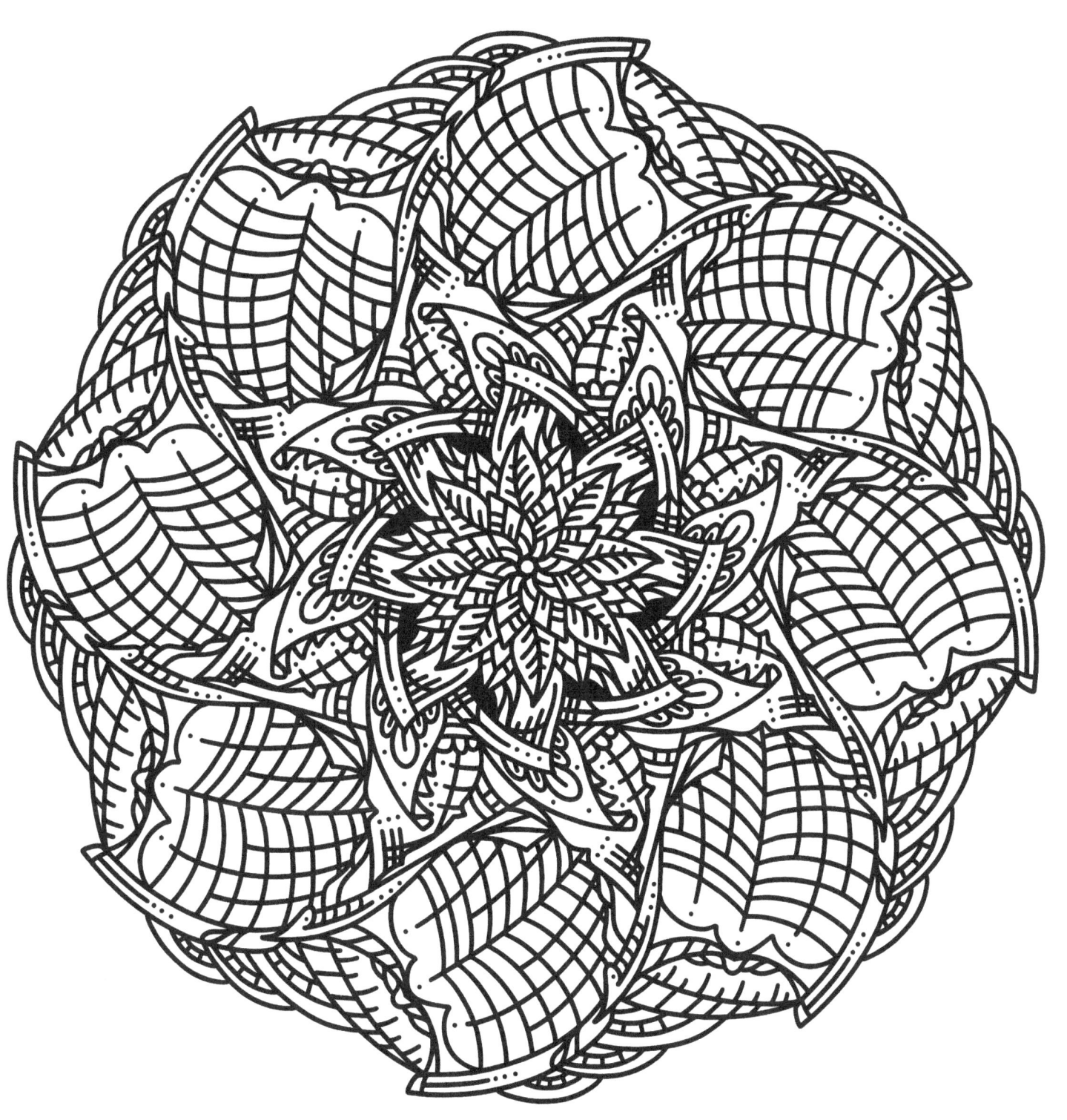

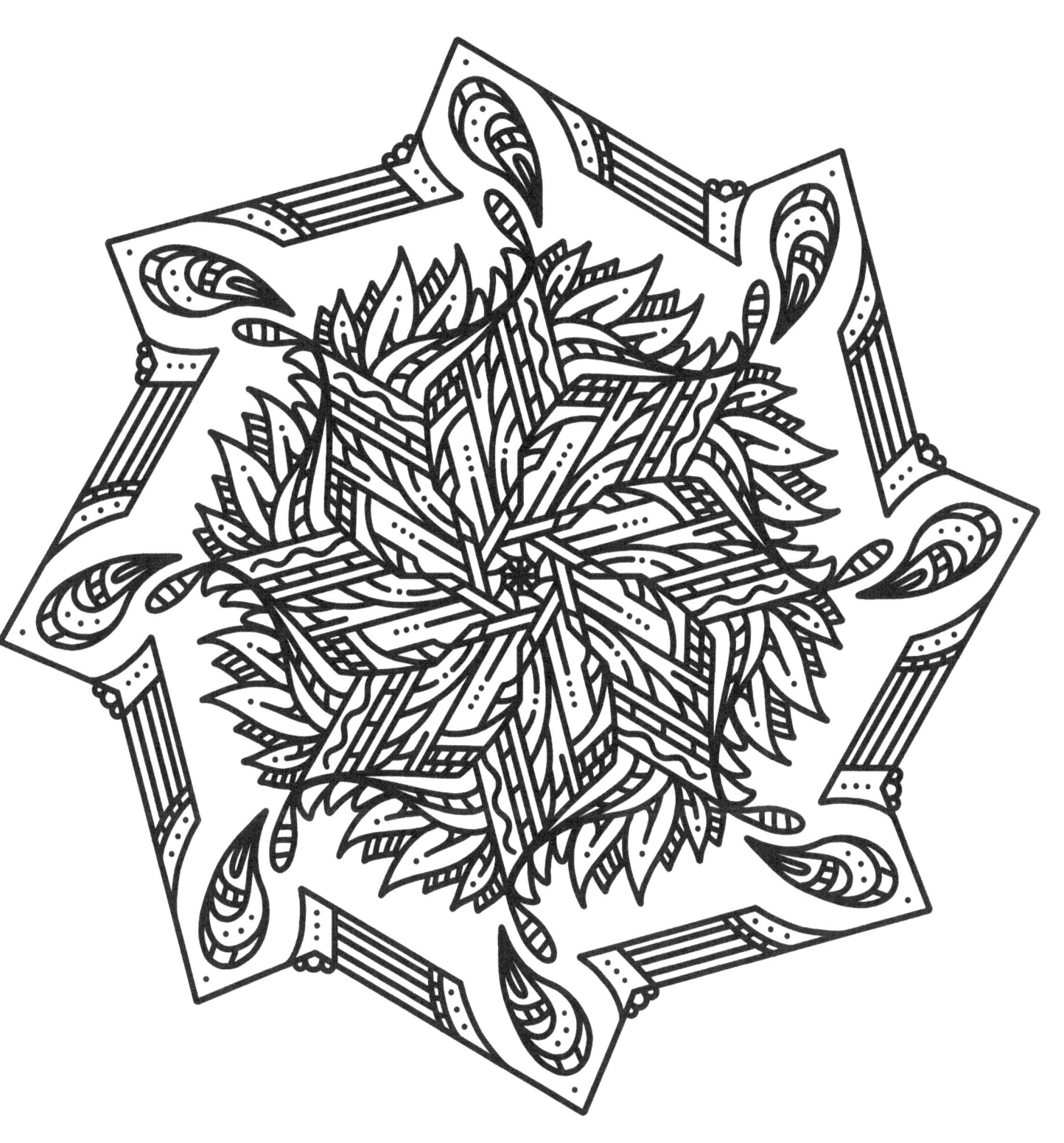

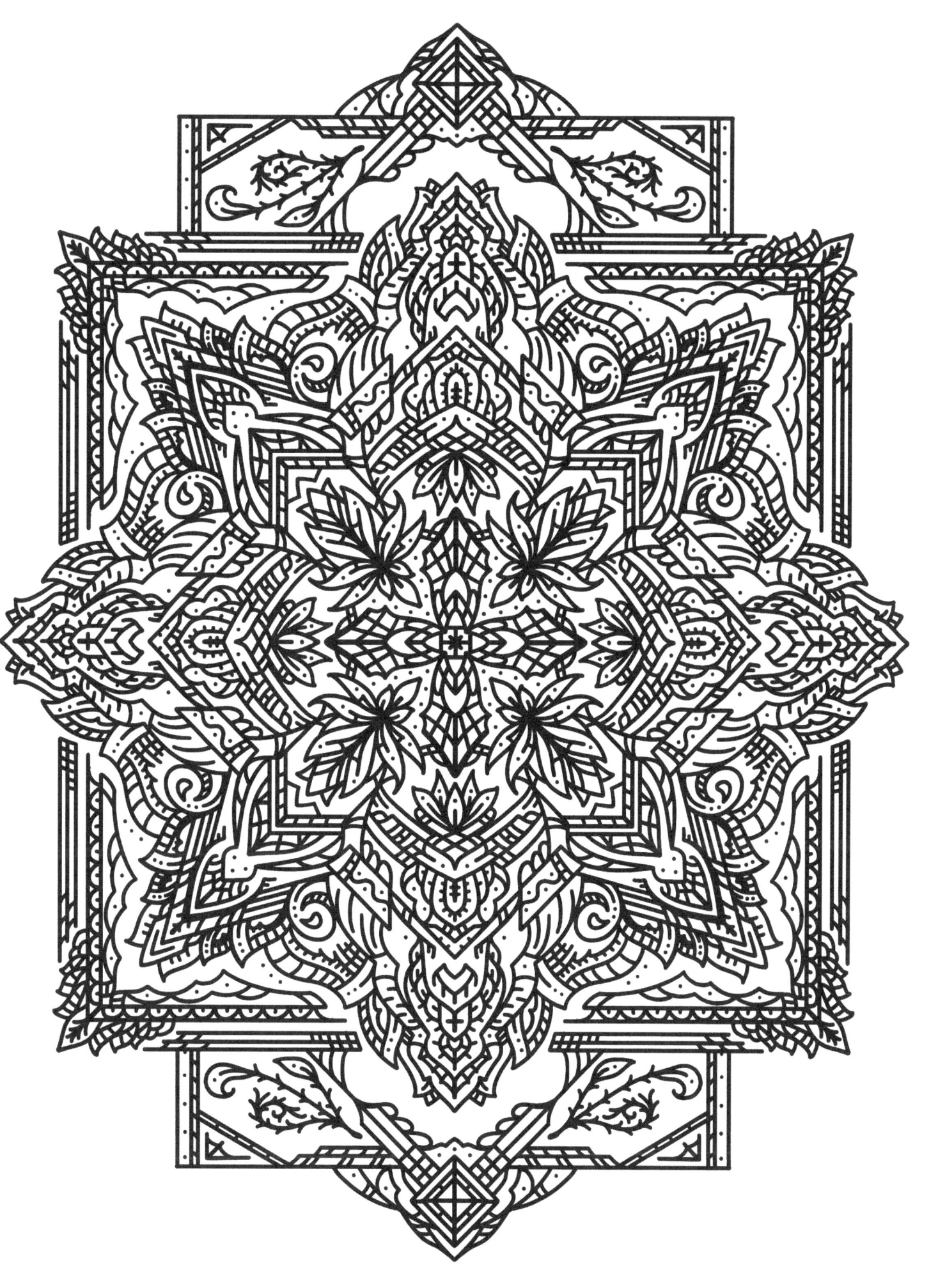

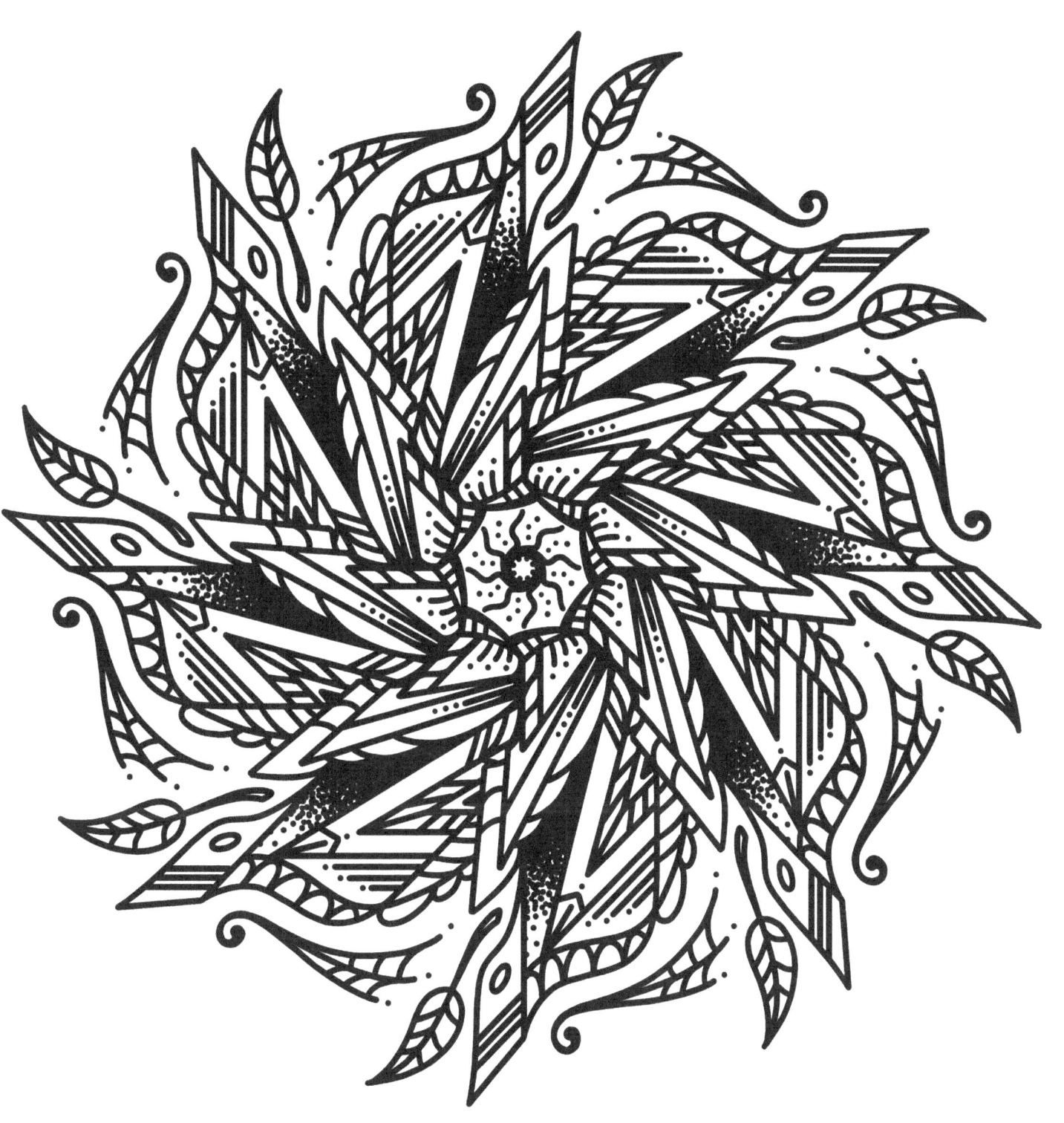

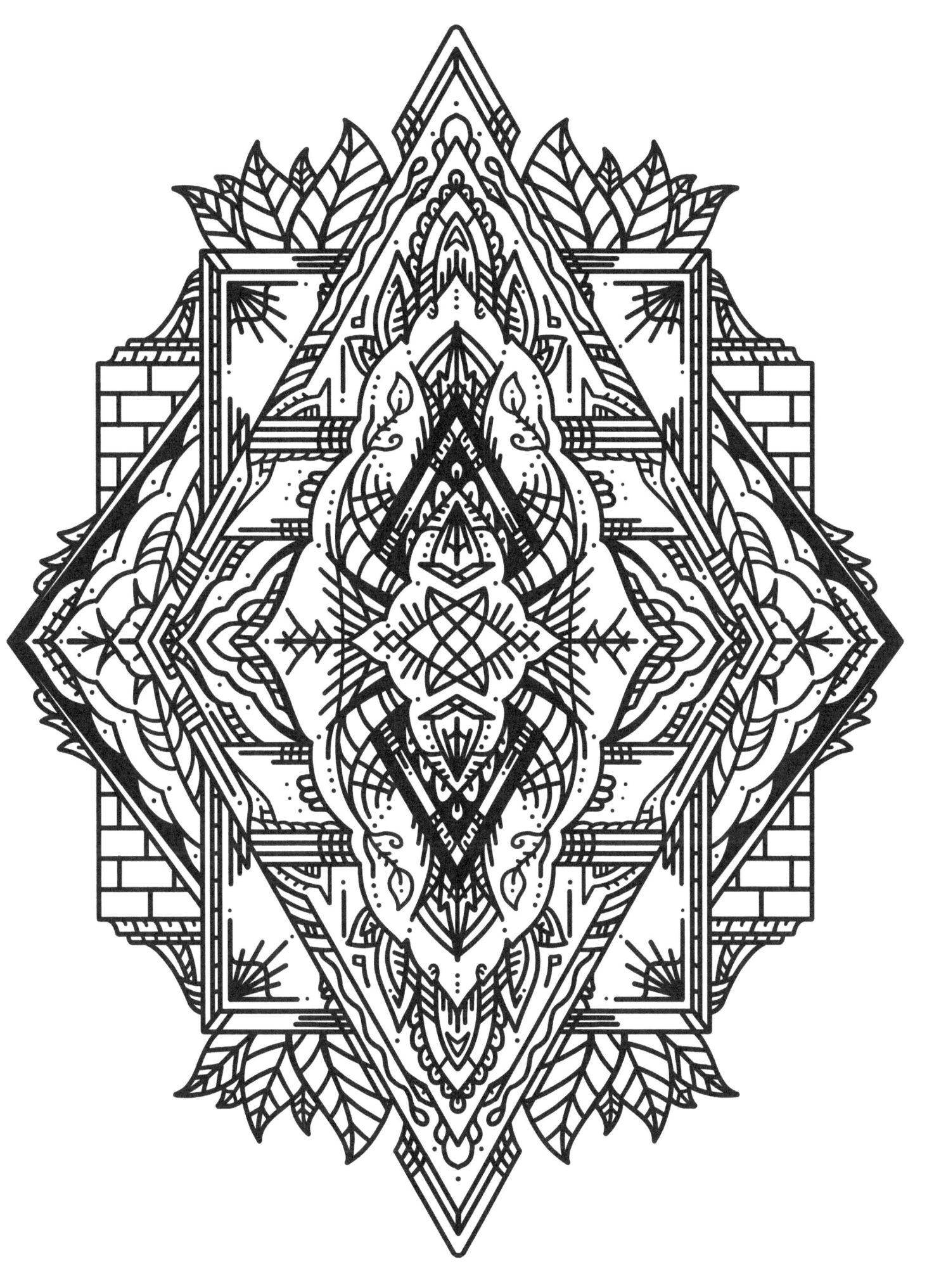

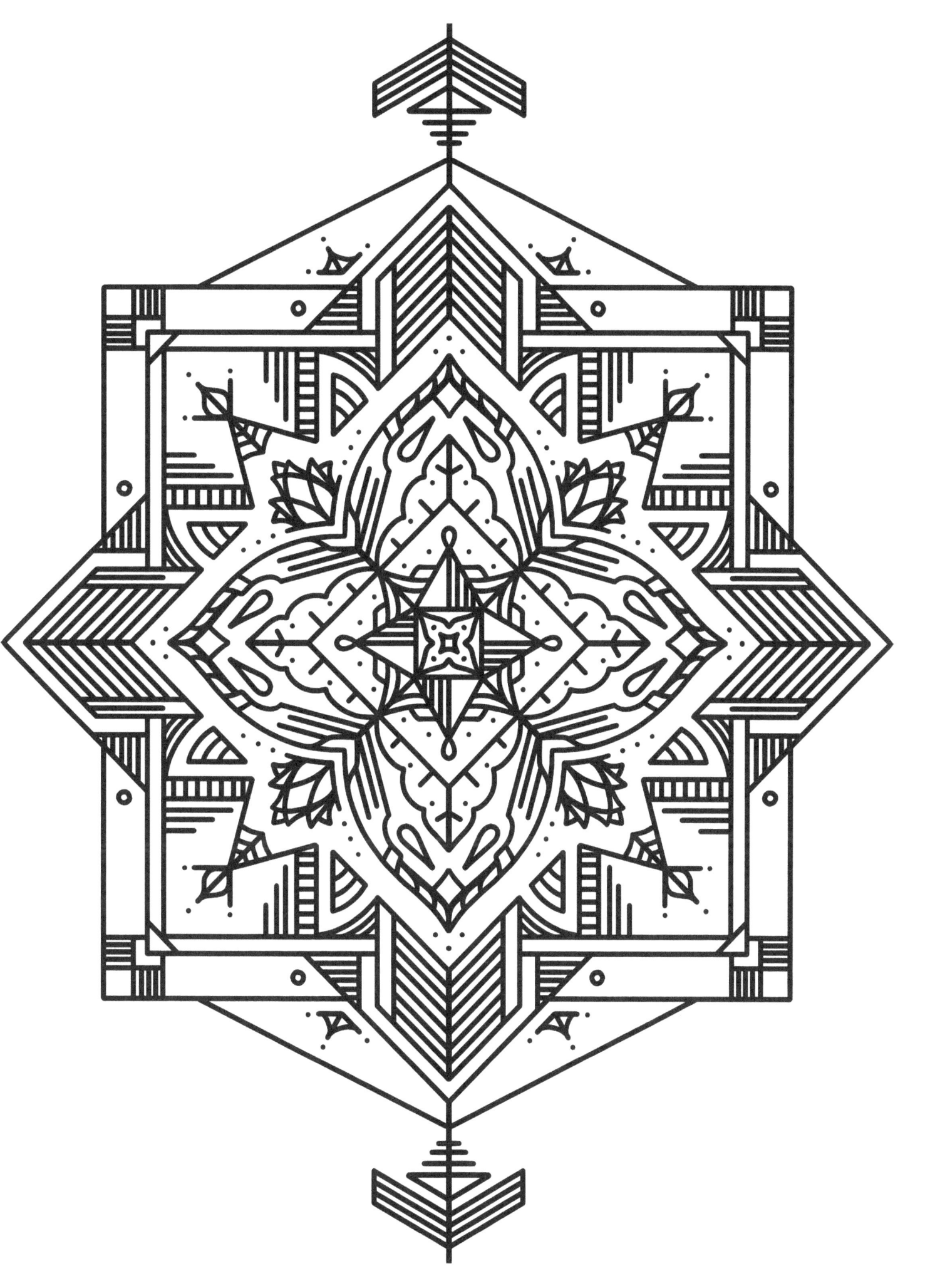

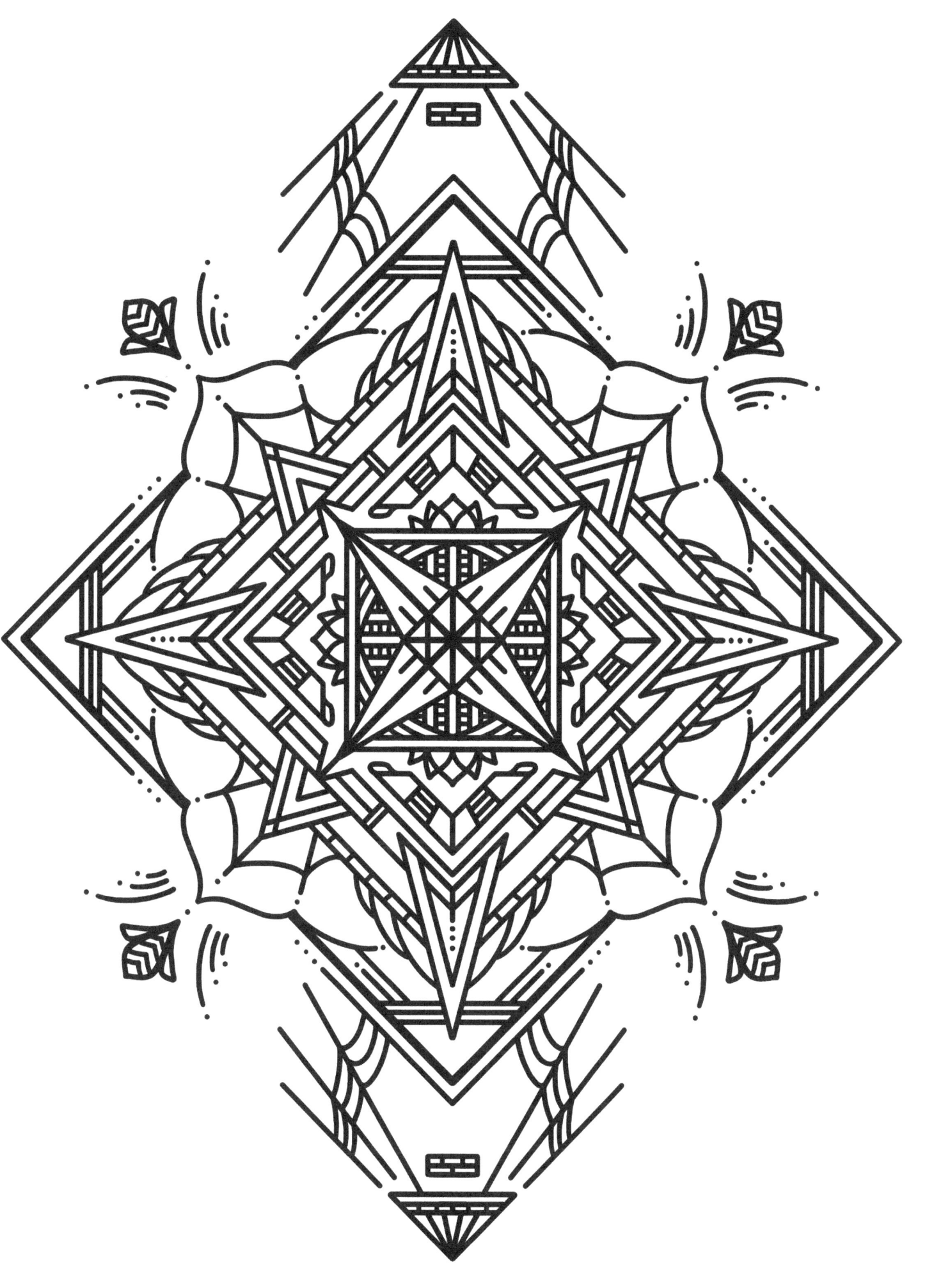

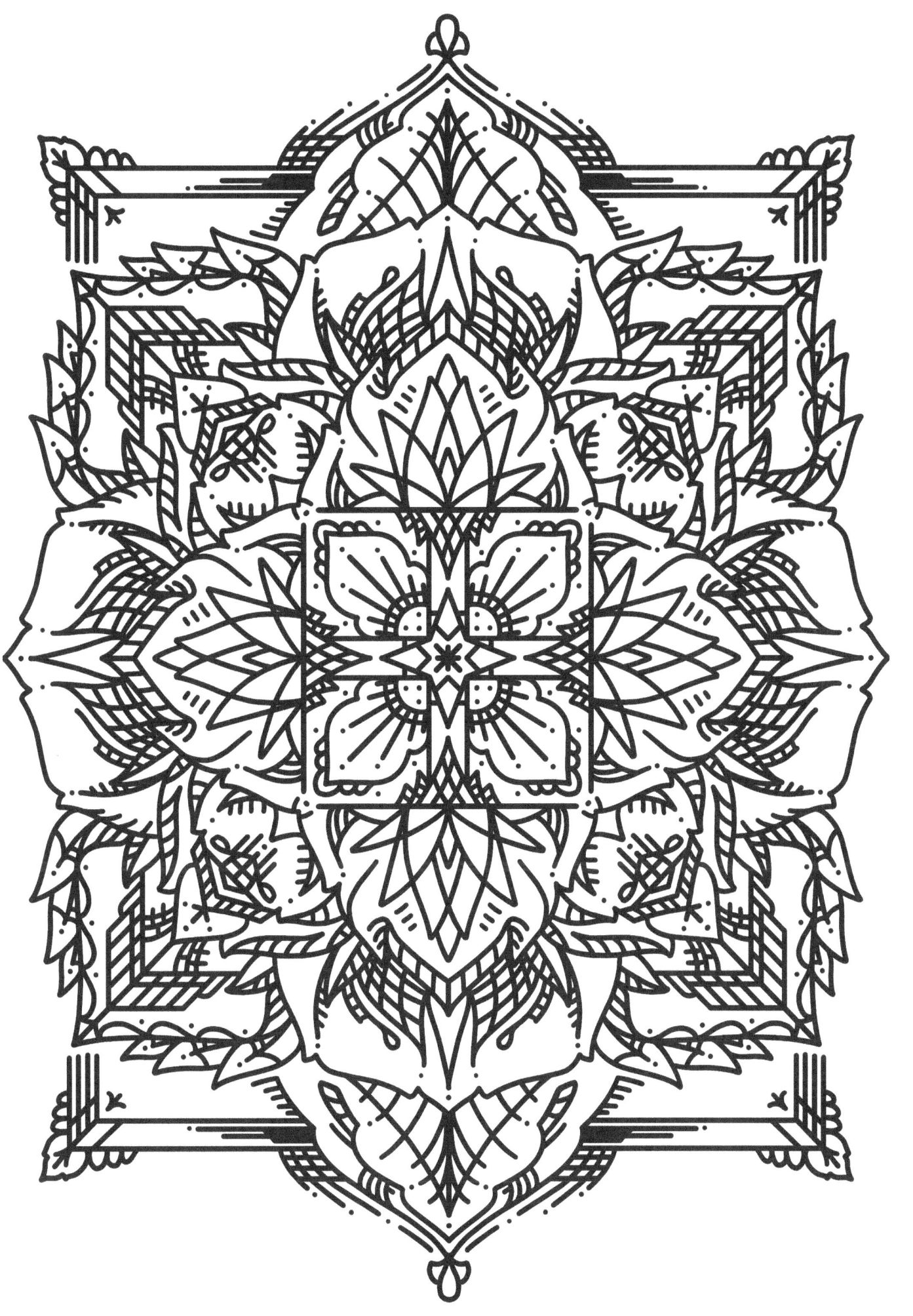

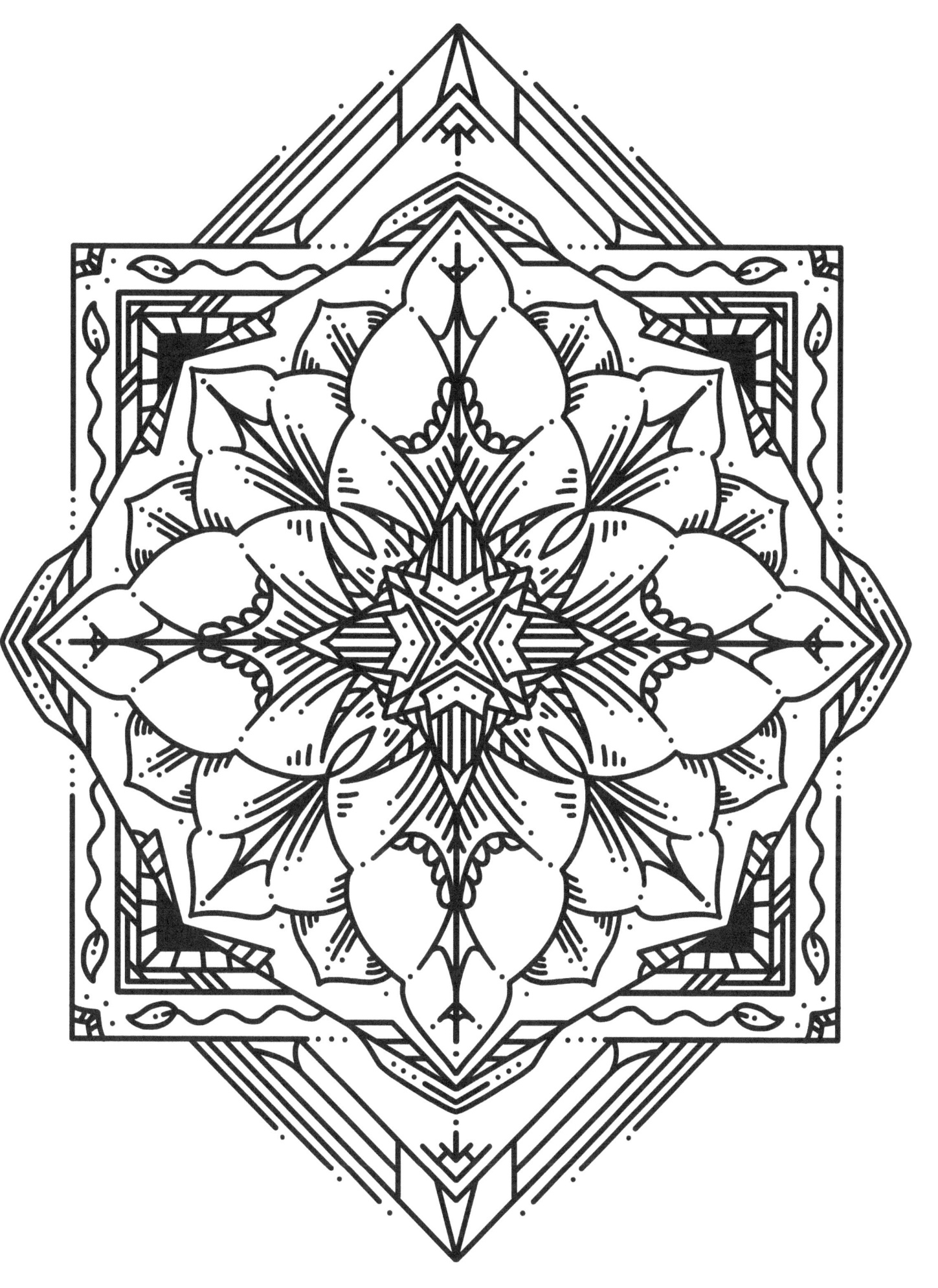

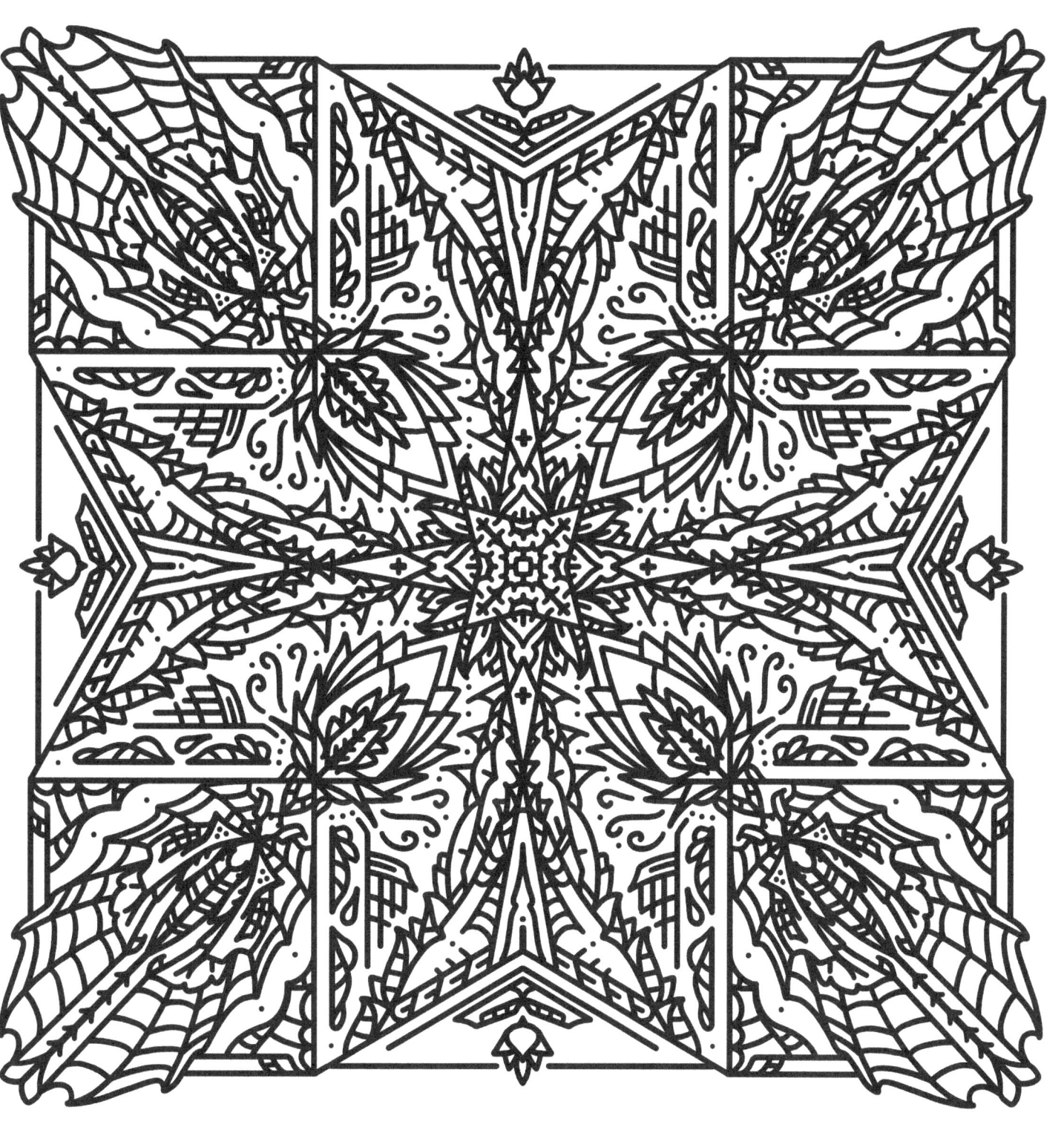

Bonus Pages

Sneak Peek Exclusive Extras

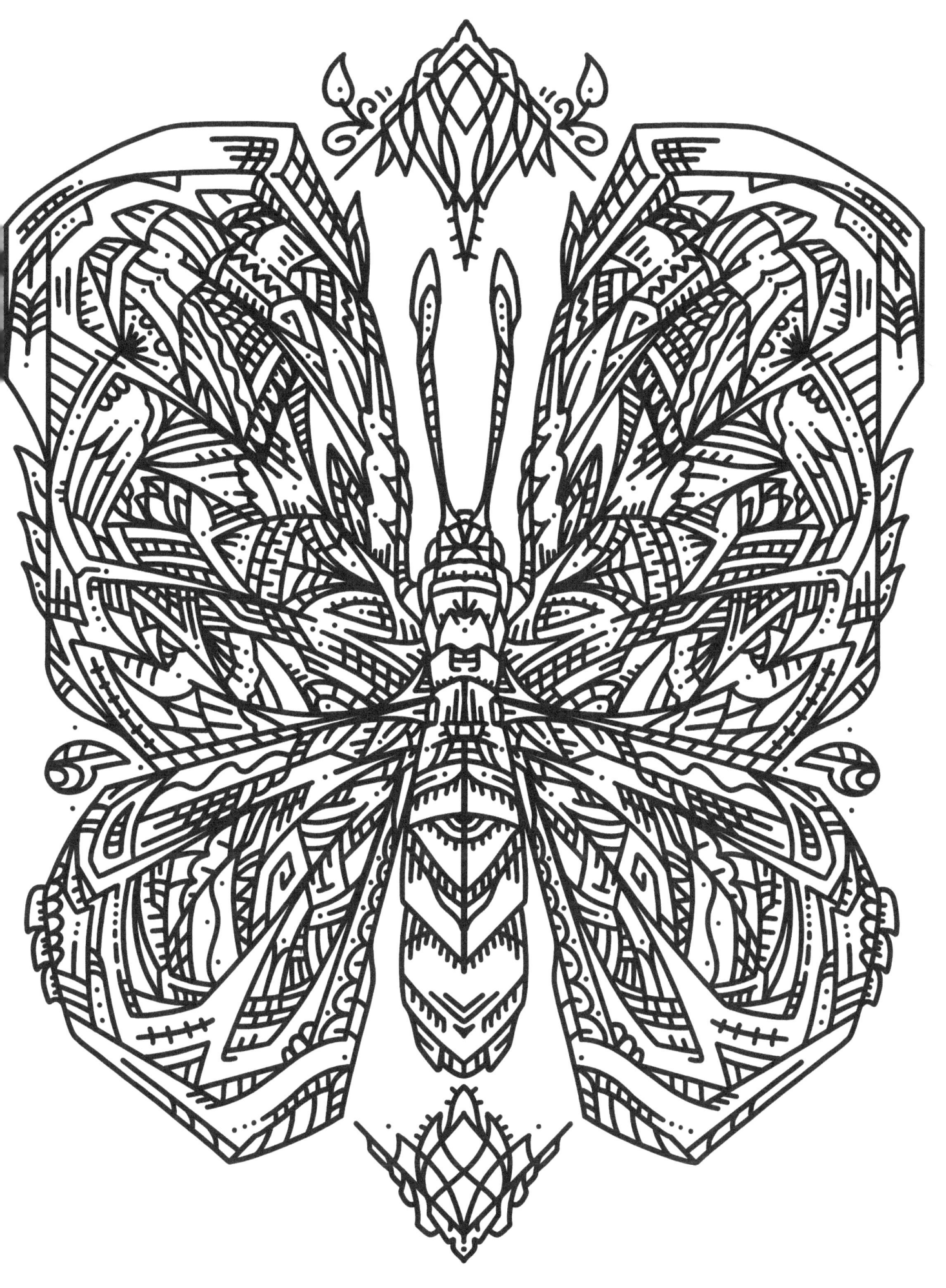

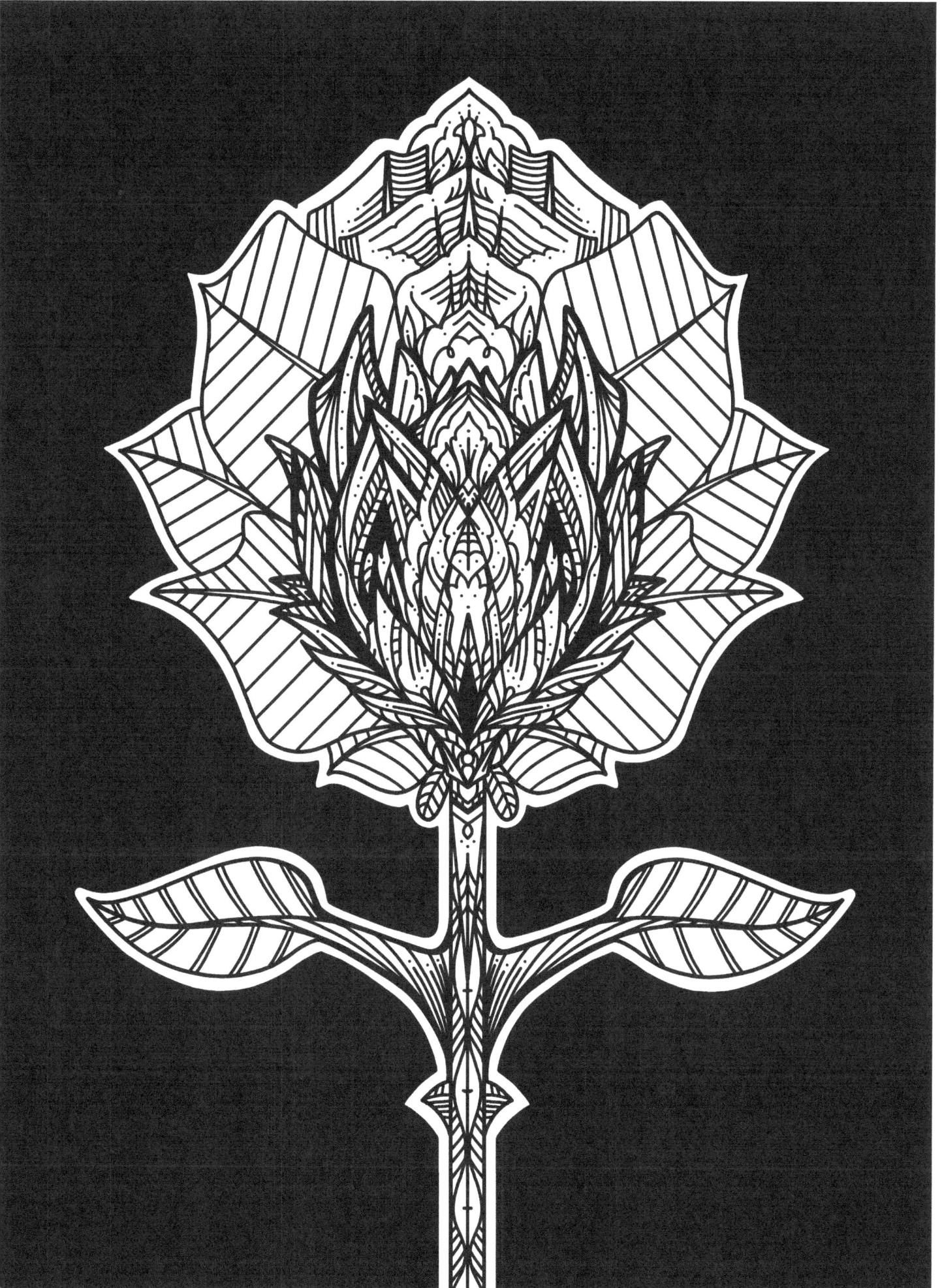

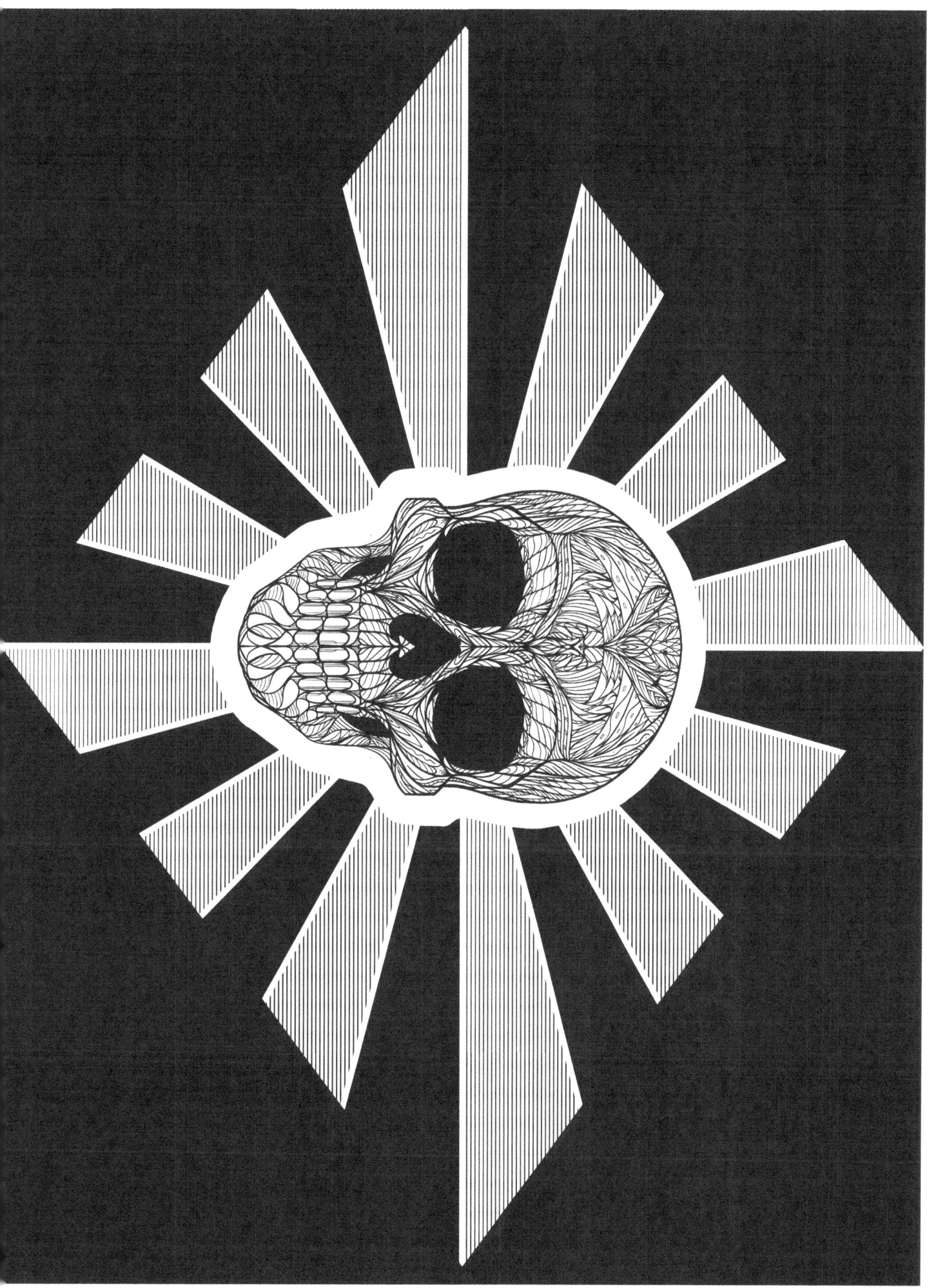